AMERICA

MW00831215

COMMUNITY SONG BOOK

FOR SCHOOLS, CLUBS ASSEMBLIES, CAMPS AND RECREATIONAL GROUPS

EDITED BY HUGO FREY

COPYRIGHT 1935 AND ASSIGNED 1988

WARNER BROS. PUBLICATIONS
Warner Music Group
An AOL Time Warner Company
15800 N.W. 48th Avenue • Miami, Florida 33014

©1984

Marching Along Together

American Lyric
by MORT DIXON

Words and Music by
EDWARD POLA and
FRANZ STEININGER
Arr. by Hugo Frey

Chorus, Snappy March tempo

K-K-K-Katy
(Male Voices)

GEOFFREY O'HARA

Anchors Aweigh
The Song of The Navy

Revised Lyric by
George D. Lottman

Capt. ALFRED H. MILES, U. S. N. (Ret.)
and CHAS. A. ZIMMERMANN

March tempo *(with precision)*

1st Tenor
2nd Tenor

Baritone
Bass

Stand Na - vy out to sea, Fight our
An - chors A - weigh, my boys

bat - tle cry;_____ We'll nev - er change our
chors A - weigh_____ Fare - well to col - lege

course, so vi - cious foe steer shy - y - y - y Roll
joys, we sail at break of day - day - day - day Through

Singin' In The Rain

From the M-G-M Picture "Hollywood Review of 1929"

Lyric by
ARTHUR FREED

Music by
NACIO HERB BROWN

walk down the lane With a hap - py re - frain, And sing-in'— just

Sing-in' In — The Rain. I'm Rain.

Blow The Man Down
(A Hoisting Chantey - Song)
Male Voices

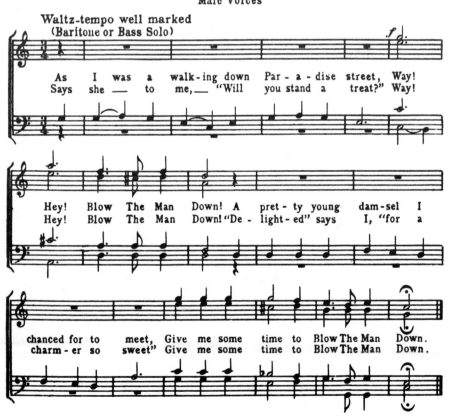

Waltz-tempo well marked
(Baritone or Bass Solo)

As I was a walk-ing down Par - a - dise street, Way!
Says she — to me, — "Will you stand a treat?" Way!

Hey! Blow The Man Down! A pret - ty young dam-sel I
Hey! Blow The Man Down! "De - light - ed" says I, "for a

chanced for to meet, Give me some time to Blow The Man Down.
charm - er so sweet" Give me some time to Blow The Man Down.

When The Moon Comes Over The Mountain

By { KATE SMITH,
HARRY WOODS and
HOWARD JOHNSON

I'm Always Chasing Rainbows

Lyric by
JOSEPH McCARTHY

Music by
HARRY CARROLL

Pagan Love Song

From the M-G-M Picture "The Pagan"

Lyric by
ARTHUR FREED

Music by
NACIO HERB BROWN

Home, Sweet Home

JOHN HOWARD PAYNE   Sir HENRY R. BISHOP

Slowly, expressive

'Mid_ pleas - ures and   pal - a - ces Though we may roam, Be it
I _ gaze _ on the   moon as I tread_ the drear wild, And_
An _ ex __ ile from home, splen-dor daz - zles in vain, Oh, —

ev - er so hum-ble, There's no _ place like home; A __ charm_ from the
feel_ that my moth-er now thinks of   her   child; As she looks_ on that
give_ me my low - ly thatched cot - tage a - gain; The_ birds_ sing-ing

skies seem to   hal __ low us   there, Which_   seek_ thro' the
moon from our   own __ cot - tage   door, Thro' the wood - bine whose
gai - ly, that came__ at my   call: Give me them__ and that

world, is ne'er met — with else - where.
fra-grance shall cheer_ me no   more.   Home, home, sweet sweet
peace of_ mind, dear_ er than all.

home, There's no — place like home, There's no_ place like home.

Auld Lang Syne

ROBERT BURNS

OLD SCOTCH AIR

1. Should auld ac-quaint-ance be for-got, And nev-er brought to mind? Should
2. We twa ha'e ran a boot the braes, And pu'd the gow - ans fine, We're
3. We twa ha'e sport- ed i' the burn Frae morn-in' sun till dine, But
4. And here's a hand my trust- y frien', And gie's a hand o' thine; We'll

auld ac-quaint-ance be for-got, And days of Auld Lang Syne?
wan-der'd mony a wea-ry foot Sin Auld Lang Syne.
seas be-tween us braid ha'e roared Sin Auld Lang Syne. For Auld Lang
tak' a cup o' kind-ness yet For Auld Lang Syne.

Syne, my dear, For Auld Lang Syne, We'll tak' a cup o' kind-ness yet, For Auld Lang Syne.

Sweet And Low

ALFRED TENNYSON

J. BARNBY

Slowly

Sweet And Low, Sweet And Low, Wind of the west - ern sea;_ Low, low,_
Sleep and rest, sleep and rest, Fa - ther will come to thee soon;_ Rest, rest on

breathe and blow, Wind of the west - ern sea;_
moth - er's breast, Fa - ther will come to thee soon;_
O-ver the roll - ing
O - ver the
Fa-ther will come to his
Fa - ther will

wa - ters go, Come from the dy - ing moon_ and blow, Blow him a-gain to
wa - ters go, Come ___ from the moon_ and blow,
babe in the nest, Sil - ver sails all out of the west, Un-der the sil - ver
come to his nest, Sil - ver sails out of _ the west,

me, _ While my lit-tle one, while my pret - ty one sleeps.
moon, _ Sleep, my lit-tle one, sleep, my pret - ty one, sleep.

The Old Oaken Bucket

SAMUEL WOODWORTH

E. KAILLMARK

How dear to my heart are the scenes of my child-hood, When fond rec-ol-
The or-chard, the mead-ow, the deep tan-gled wild-wood, And ev-'ry loved

Chorus: The Old Oak-en Buck-et the i - ron bound buck-et, The moss cov-ered

Fine

lec-tion pre-sents them to view! The wide spread-ing pond, and the mill that stood
spot which my in - fan-cy knew:

buck-et that hung in the well.

by it, The bridge and the rock where the cat-a-ract fell; The cot of my

fa-ther, the dai-ry house nigh it, And e'en the rude buck-et that hung in the well.

Old Black Joe

STEPHEN C. FOSTER

1. Gone are the days when my heart was young and gay; Gone are my friends from the cot-ton fields a-way; Gone from the earth to a bet-ter land I know, I hear their gen-tle voi-ces call-ing, "Old Black Joe!"

2. Why do I weep when my heart should feel no pain? Why do I sigh that my friends come not a-gain? Griev-ing for forms now de-part-ed long a-go, I hear their gen-tle voi-ces call-ing, "Old Black Joe!"

3. Where are the hearts once so hap-py and so free? The chil-dren so dear that I held up-on my knee? Gone to the shore where my soul has longed to go, I hear their gen-tle voi-ces call-ing, "Old Black Joe!"

Refrain

I'm com-ing, I'm com-ing, For my head is bend-ing low; I hear those gen-tle voi-ces call-ing, "Old Black Joe!"

Old Folks At Home

STEPHEN C. FOSTER

Moderate, with expression

1. { 'Way down up-on de Swa-nee Riv - er, Far, far a - way,
All up and down de whole cre - a - tion, Sad - ly I roam,

2. { All roun' de lit - tle farm I wan-dered, When I was young;
When I was play-ing with my broth - er, Hap - py was I;

3. { One lit - tle hut a - mong de bush - es, One that I love,
When will I see de bees a - hum-ming, All roun' de comb?

Dere's wha my heart is turn-ing ev - er, Dere's wha de old folks stay. }
Still long-ing for de old plan-ta - tion, And for de old folks at home. }

Den man - y hap - py days I squan-dered, Man - y de songs I ___ sung. }
Oh! take me to my kind old moth - er, There let me live and die. }

Still sad - ly to my mem-'ry rush - es, No mat-ter where I ___ rove. }
When will I hear de ban - jo tum-ming, Down in my good old home? }

Refrain

optional

mf
All de world is sad and drear-y, Ev-'ry-where I roam; Hm

Oh! dark-ies, how my heart grows wear-y, Far from de Old Folks At Home.

Love's Old Sweet Song

C. CLIFTON BINGHAM

J. L. MOLLOY

Moderate, without dragging

mp

Once in the dear dead days be-yond re-call, When on the world the mists be-gan to fall,
E-ven to-day we hear love's song of yore, Deep in our hearts it dwells for-ev-er-more,

Out of the dreams that rose in hap-py throng, Low to our hearts love sang an old sweet song,
Foot-steps may fal-ter, wear-y grow the way, Still we can hear it at the close of day,

And in the dusk, Where fell the fire-light gleam, Soft-ly it wove it-self in-to our dream.
So till the end, When life's dim shadows fall, Love will be found the sweet-est song of all.

Refrain

mp

Just a song at twi-light When the lights are low And the flick-'ring shad-ows

soft-ly come and go;— Tho' the heart be wear-y Sad the day and long

Still to us at twi-light comes love's old song, Comes Love's Old Sweet Song.

In The Gloaming

META ORRED

ANNIE F. HARRISON

Slowly

mp

1. In The Gloam-ing oh, my dar-ling! when the lights are dim and low,
2. In The Gloam-ing oh, my dar-ling! think not bit - ter - ly of me!

rall.

And the qui - et shad - ows, fall-ing, soft - ly come and soft-ly go,
Though I pass'd a - way in si-lence, left you lone-ly, set you free,

animated

When the winds are sob - bing faint-ly with a gen - tle, un-known woe,
For my heart was crush'd with long-ing; what had been could nev - er be.

a tempo

Will you think of me and love me, As you did once long a - go?
It was best to leave you thus, dear, Best for you and best for

2. *rall.* *cresc.*

me, It was best to leave you thus,— Best for you and best for me.—

Long, Long Ago

THOS. HAYNES BAYLEY

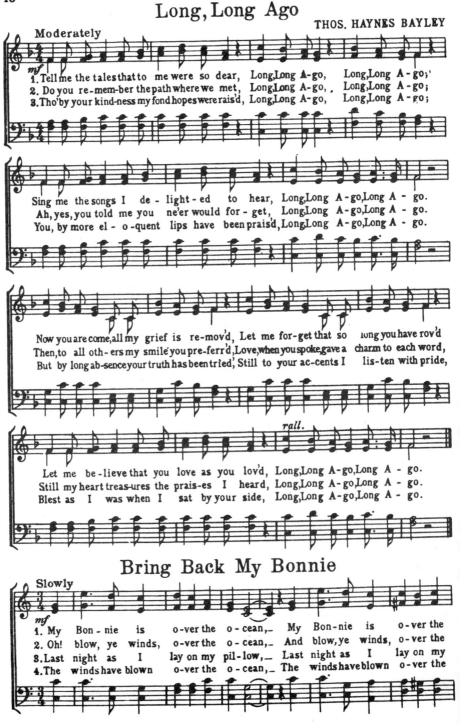

Bring Back My Bonnie

The Lonesome Road

Silver Threads Among The Gold

H.P. DANKS

Slowly

1. Dar-ling, I am grow-ing old;— Sil - ver Threads A-mong The Gold
2. When your hair is sil - ver white. And your cheeks no long- er bright
3. Love can nev - er more grow old;— Locks may lose their brown and gold,
4. Love is al -ways young and fair.— What to us is sil - ver hair,

Shine up - on my brow to - day;— Life is fad-ing fast a - way;
With the ro - ses of the May,— I will kiss your lips and say:
Cheeks may fade and hol - low grow;— But the hearts that love will know
Fad - ed cheeks or steps grown slow,— To the hearts that beat be - low?

But, my dar-ling, you will be, will be, Al-ways young and fair to me,
Oh! my dar-ling, mine a - lone, a - lone, You have nev - er old- er grown,—
Nev - er, nev - er win-ter's frost and chill; Sum-mer warmth is in them still,—
Since I kiss'd you, mine a - lone, a - lone, You have nev - er old- er grown,—

Yes! my dar-ling, you will be,— Al-ways young and fair to me.
Yes! my dar-ling, mine a - lone,— You have nev - er old- er grown.
Nev - er win-ter's frost and chill,— Sum-mer warmth is in them still.—
Since I kiss'd you, mine a - lone,— You have nev - er old- er grown.—

Refrain

Dar-ling, I am grow-ing old, —— Sil-ver Threads A-mong The Gold.

Shine up-on my brow to - day,— Life is fad-ing fast a - way.

My Old Kentucky Home

STEPHEN C. FOSTER

Slowly, with expression

1. {The sun shines bright in the old Ken-tuck-y home, 'Tis sum-mer, the dark-ies are
young folks roll on the lit-tle cab-in floor, All mer-ry all hap-py and
2. {They hunt no more for the pos-sum and the coon, On the mead-ow the hill and the
day goes by like a shad-ow o'er the heart, With sor-row where all was de-
3. {The head must bow and the back will have to bend, Where-ev-er the dark-y may
few more days for to tote the wea-ry load, No mat-ter 'twill nev-er be

gay; The corn tops ripe and the mead-ows in the bloom, While the
bright; By'n by hard times comes a knock-ing at the door, Then my
shore; They sing no more by the glim-mer of the moon, On the
light; The time has come when the dark-ies have to part, Then my
go, A few more days, and the troub-le all will end, In the
light, A few more days till we tot-ter on the road, Then my

1. birds make_ mu-sic all the day. The Old Ken-tuck-y Home, good-night.
2. bench by the old_ cab-in door. The Old Ken-tuck-y Home, good-night.
3. field where the su-gar-canes grow. A Old Ken-tuck-y Home, good-night.

Chorus

Weep no more my la-dy, O weep no more to-day! We will sing one song for the

Old Ken-tuck-y Home, For the Old Ken-tuck-y Home, far a-way.

Carry Me Back To Old Virginny

JAMES A. BLAND

Slowly

Car-ry Me Back To Old Vir-gin-ny, There's where the cot-ton and the

corn and 'ta-toes grow, There's where the birds war-ble sweet in the spring-time,

rit. Fine

There's where the old dar-key's heart am longed to go.—

Fine

mf

There's where I la-bored so__ hard for old Mas-sa, Day af-ter day in the

field of yel-low corn, No place on earth do I love more sin-cere-ly

Billy Boy

The Little Brown Church

Wᵐ S. PITTS

GEO. COOPER

Sweet Genevieve

HENRY TUCKER

Slowly, expressive

O, Gen-e-vieve I'd give the world To live a-gain the love-ly past! The
Fair Gen-e-vieve my ear-ly love, The years but make thee dear-er far! My

rose of youth was dew im-pearled, But how it with-ers in the blast. I
heart shall nev-er, nev-er rove: Thou art my on-ly guid-ing star, For

see thy face in ev-'ry dream, My wak-ing tho'ts are full of thee; Thy
me the past has no re-gret, What-e'er the years may bring to me; I

glance is in the star-ry beam That falls a-long the sum-mer sea.
bless the hour when first we met, The hour that gave me love and thee! } O,

Refrain

Gen-e-vieve, Sweet Gen-e-vieve, The days may come the days may go, But

still the hands of mem-'ry weave The bliss-ful dreams of long a-go.

Grandfather's Clock

HENRY C. WORK

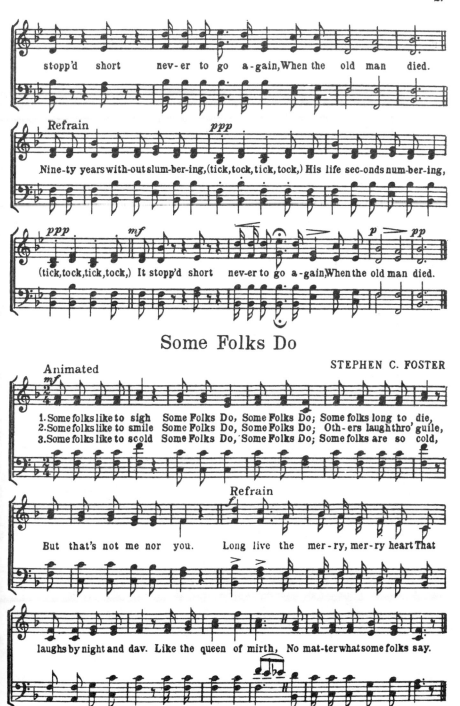

stopp'd short nev-er to go a-gain, When the old man died.

Refrain *ppp*

Nine-ty years with-out slum-ber-ing, (tick, tock, tick, tock,) His life sec-onds num-ber-ing,

ppp *mf* *p* *pp*

(tick, tock, tick, tock,) It stopp'd short nev-er to go a-gain, When the old man died.

Some Folks Do

STEPHEN C. FOSTER

Animated
mf

1. Some folks like to sigh   Some Folks Do, Some Folks Do; Some folks long to die,
2. Some folks like to smile   Some Folks Do, Some Folks Do; Oth-ers laugh thro' guile,
3. Some folks like to scold   Some Folks Do, Some Folks Do; Some folks are so cold,

Refrain
f

But that's not me nor you.   Long live the mer-ry, mer-ry heart That

laughs by night and day. Like the queen of mirth, No mat-ter what some folks say.

Bonnie Eloise

C.W. ELLIOTT

J.R. THOMAS

Slowly

O,— sweet is the vale where the Mo-hawk gent-ly glides On its
O,— sweet are the scenes of my boy-hood's sun-ny years That be-
O,— sweet are the mo-ments when dream - ing I roam Thru my

clear wind - ing way to the sea _____ And —
span - gle the gay val - ley o'er _____ And —
loved haunts now mos - sy and gray _____ And —

(to the sea)
(val - ley o'er)
(now so gray)

dear - er than all sto - ried streams on earth be - sides Is this
dear are the friends seen thru mem - o - ries' fond tears That have
dear - er than all is my child-hood's hal - low'd home That is

Refrain

bright roll - ing riv - er to me _____ But
lived in the blest days of yore _____
crumb - ling now slow - ly a - way _____

(to me,)
(of yore)
(a - way)

sweet - er, dear - er, yes, dear - er far than these Who

charm where oth-ers all fail, Is blue-eyed, Bon-nie,

Bon-nie E-lo-ise, The Belle of the Mo-hawk Vale.

I've Been Wukkin' On De Railroad

Marcia

I've Been Wuk-kin'On De Rail-road All de live long day;_ I've Been Wuk-kin On De

Rail-road, To pass de time a-way._ Doan' yo'hyar de whis-tle blow-in',

Rise up so ear-ly in the mawn; Doan' yo'hyar de cap-n'shout-in!"Di-nah,blow yo' hawn!"

Lovely Evening
(Round)

Oh, how love-ly is the eve-ning, is the eve-ning,When the bells are

sweet-ly ring-ing, sweet-ly ring-ing! Ding, dong, ding, dong, ding, dong.

De Camptown Races

STEPHEN C. FOSTER.

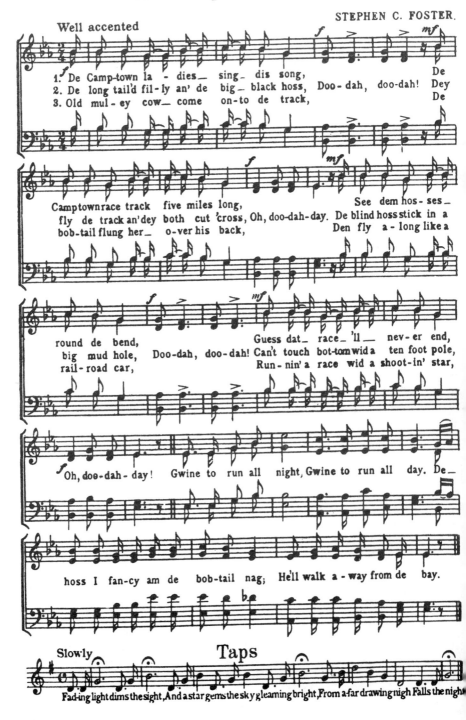

Well accented

1. De Camp-town la - dies— sing— dis song, De
2. De long tail'd fil-ly an' de big— black hoss, Doo-dah, doo-dah! Dey
3. Old mul-ey cow— come on-to de track, De

Camptown race track five miles long, See dem hos-ses—
fly de track an'dey both cut 'cross, Oh, doo-dah-day. De blind hoss stick in a
bob-tail flung her— o-ver his back,

round de bend, Guess dat— race— 'll nev-er end,
big mud hole, Doo-dah, doo-dah! Can't touch bot-tom wid a ten foot pole,
rail-road car, Run-nin' a race wid a shoot-in' star,

Oh, doo-dah-day! Gwine to run all night, Gwine to run all day. De—

Den fly a-long like a

hoss I fan-cy am de bob-tail nag; He'll walk a-way from de bay.

Slowly   **Taps**

Fad-ing light dims the sight, And a star gems the sky gleaming bright, From a-far drawing nigh Falls the night

Massa's In De Cold Ground

Slowly

STEPHEN C. FOSTER

1. Round de mead-ows am a - ring-ing, De dark-ey's mourn-ful
2. When de au - tumn leaves were fall - in; When de days were
3. Mas - sa make de dark - eys love him, Cayse he was so

song, While de mock-ing bird am sing-ing, Hap-py as de day am
cold, 'Twas hard to hear old mas-sa call-ing, Cayse he was so weak and
kind, Now, dey sad - ly weep a - bove him, Mourning cayse he leave dem be-

long, While de i - vy am a - creep-ing, O'er de grass-y mound,
old, Now de or-ange trees am bloom-ing, On de sand-y shore,
hind, I can not work be-fore to - mor - row, Cayse de tear drop flow; I

Dare old mas-sa am a - sleep-ing, Sleep-ing in de cold, cold ground.
Now de sum-mer days am com - ing, Mas - sa neb-ber calls no more.
try to drive a-way my sor - row, Pick- in' on de old ban - jo.

Chorus

Down in de corn - field Hear dat mourn - ful sound;

rit.

All de dark-eys am a - weep-ing, Mas-sa's In De Cold, Cold Ground.

In The Time Of Roses

LUISE REICHARDT

Slowly, with expression

1. In The Time Of Ros - es   Hope, thou wea - ry heart!   When the blooms un -
2. In The Time Of Ros - es   Wea - ry heart re - joice!   Ere the sum - mer

clos - es, Thou, too rest thy heart   Tho' thy grief___   o'er comes thee, Thru ___
clos - es, Comes the longed-for voice   Let not death ___   ap - pal thee, For ___

___ the win - ter's gloom Thou shalt thrust it from thee, When The Ros - es Bloom.
___ be - yond the tomb, God, him - self shall call thee, When The Ros - es Bloom.

Comin' 'Thro' The Rye

FOLK SONG

Moderately

1.   If a bod - y meet a bod - y, Com - in' Thro' The Rye,   If a bod - y
2.   If a bod - y meet a bod - y, Com - in' frae the town,   If a bod - y
3. A - mang the train there is a swain I dear - ly love my - sel, But what's his name, or

Chorus

kiss a bod - y   need a bod - y   cry?
greet a bod - y   need a bod - y   frown?   Ev - 'ry las - sie has her lad - die,
where's his hame, I   din - na choose to   tell.

Nane, they say, ha'e I; Yet a' the lads they smile on me, When Com-in'Thro' The Rye.

Nellie Was A Lady

STEPHEN C. FOSTER

Moderately

1. Down on the Mis-sis-sip-pi float-ing, Long time I trav-el on the
2. Now I'm un-hap-py and I'm weep-ing, Can't tote the cot-ton-wood no
3. Down in the mead-ow 'mong the clo-ver, Walk with my Nel-lie by my

way; All night the cot-ton-wood a - tot-ing
more; Last night when Nel-lie was a - sleep-ing
side; Now all those hap-py days are o - ver,

Refrain

Sing for my true love all the day.
Death came a-knock-ing at the door.
Fare-well, my dark Vir-gin-ny bride.

Nel-lie Was A La-dy,

Last night she died; Toll the bell for love-ly Nell, My dark Vir-gin-ny bride.

84

Captain Jinks

Sailing

GODFREY MARKS

Brightly
f

Sail-ing, Sail-ing, o-ver the bound-ing main, For man-y a storm-y
wind shall blow ere Jack comes home a-gain. Sail-ing, Sail-ing, o-ver the bound-ing

(ad lib. rit.)

main; For man-y a storm-y wind shall blow ere Jack comes home a-gain.

The Curtains Of Night

COWBOY SONG

Moderately
mf

When The Cur-tains Of Night are pinned back by the stars, And the
When The Cur-tains Of Night are pinned back by the stars, And the

beau-ti-ful moon sweeps the sky, I'll re-mem-ber you, Love, in my prayers.
dew drops of heav'n kiss the rose, I'll re-mem-ber you, Love, in my prayers.

Dream Faces

W. M. HUTCHINSON

Slowly

1. The shad-ows lie a - cross the dim old room, The fire-light glows and
2. more I see a - cross the dis-tant years A face, long gone with

fades in - to the gloom, While mem - 'ry sails to child-hood's dis-tant
all its smiles and tears, Once more I press a ten - der, lov-ing

shore, And dreams, and dreams of days that are no more.
hand. And with my dar - ling 'neath the old oak stand.

Allegro (Flowing)

Sweet dream-land fa-ces, pass-ing to and fro,__ Bring back to

mem - 'ry days of long a - go__ Mur - mur - ing gent-ly

to Coda

thru a mist of pain._ "Hope on, dear loved one, we shall meet a-

gain." 2.Once _gain." 3.But all I loved are gone, And I a-lone in

life, To wait, and wait, and wait,—'Till death shall end the strife; Un-

til once more I join The hearts that loved me best, Where the

I join —— The hearts that loved me best,

wick-ed cease from troub-ling, And the wea-ry are at rest.—

We shall meet a-gain.—— We shall meet, shall meet a-gain.——

Beautiful Isle Of The Sea

GEORGE COOPER

J.R. THOMAS

Moderately

Beau-ti-ful Isle Of The Sea! Smile on the brow of the
Oft on your shell gird-led shore, Eve - ning has found me re-

The beau-ti-ful
Your shore,

wa - ters, Dear are your mem-'ries to me,
clin - ing, Vi - sions of youth dream-ing o'er,

Sweet as the songs of your daught-ers; O - ver your moun-tains and
Down where the light-house was shin - ing; Far from the glad-ness you

vales,
gave,

Down by each mur - mur-ing
Far from all joys worth pos-

O - ver your moun-tains and vales. Down by each
Far from the glad-ness you gave. Far from all

riv - er, Cheered by the flow'r lov-ing gales,
sess - ing, Still o'er the lone wea-ry wave,

mur - mur-ing riv - er.
joys worth pos-sess - ing.

When The Lights Are Low

GERALD M. LANE

Brightly

When twi-light falls on the dim old walls, And day is past and done; As we
With dis-tant sounds in the streets a-round, The throng goes surg-ing by; But

sit and dream in the fad - ing gleam, Come mem-'ries one by one.
far a - way in dreams we stray, Where ver-dant mead-ows lie.

Old friends known in the years long gone. In fan - cy greet us still, And
There once more, as in days of yore, To roam each well-known way, 'Till

rall.

voi - ces dear, that we long to hear, The si - lence seem to fill.
o - ver all night's shad-ows fall, And dream-land fades a - way.

Allegretto

Just when the day is o - ver, Just When The Lights Are Low,

Back to the heart re - turn-eth Life's gold-en long a - go.

Far, far a - way we wan - der, Watch-ing the fire - light gleams;_

Far, far a - way from the world's shad-ows grey, In-to the land of dreams._

In The Evening By The Moonlight

JAMES A. BLAND

Moderately

In The Ev'-ning By The Moon-light, You could hear those dark-ies sing-ing In The

Ev'-ning By The Moon-light You could hear those ban-jos ring-ing How the

old folks would en - joy it, They would sit all night and lis-ten, As we

sang In The Ev' - ning By The Moon - light._

The Little Old Red Shawl My Mother Wore

CHARLES MORELAND

It now lies on the shelf, it is fad - ed and torn, That
Oh, my heart of - ten aches, with a dull throb - bing pain, When

dear old shawl my moth-er wore,—— 'Tis— all that is left for this
child-hood vis-ions come a - gain—— And— sad-ly I think of the

moth-er wore,
come a-gain

heart to a - dore, To bring to mind those hap-py days of
days that are past, Too joy - ous and too beau-ti - ful to

yore;— How of-ten the hands to these folds have been pressed, That
last;— Oh, fond, love-ly child-hood, made bright by the smile Of

now be - neath the dai - sies are at rest (at — rest) The
one whose love could ev - 'ry care be-guile (be — guile) How

tears come un-bid-den and si-lent-ly, fall, To
glad-ly I'd fly from the world's bit-ter thrall, To

rall.

gleam like gems on moth-er's old red shawl. ___
seek the heart that throbb'd be-neath this shawl. ___

Refrain
mf a tempo

It is use-ful no more, Yet I fond-ly a-dore That

dear old shawl my moth-er wore, ___ And thru life it shall be a loved

trea-sure to me, That Lit-tle Old Red Shawl My Moth-er Wore. ___

Here's To
Round

1

2

Here's a health to all them that we love! _ Here's a health to all them that love us. _

3

4

Here's a health to all them that love those that love them, That love those that love them that love us.

Good-Night, Farewell

F. KUCKEN

Moderate, animated

1. Good-night, Fare - well, my own true heart, A thou-sand times good-night!—
2. I see thy heart re - flect - ed by A star with-in— the stream,—

— Each tho't of thee bids grief de-part, And ren - ders joy more bright. Tho'
— It shines forth from thy clear, blue eye, And sheds o'er me its beam; And

poco animato   *sempre cres.*   *cresc.*

far thy im - age dwells with me, Thou art my guid-ing star;— When
tho' no more than one bright glance I e'er of thee pos - sessed,— That

o'er— me dark-ning clouds I see, Thy love guides me a - far.— When
look— my heart will e'er en - trance, And ren - der ev - er blest.— That

o'er me dark-ning clouds I see, Thy love— guides me a - far. Fare-well,—
look my heart will e'er en - trance, And ren - der ev - er blest. Fare-well,—

own true heart, A thou-sand times fare-well! Good-night, Fare-well, my own true heart!

Roll On, Silver Moon

J. W. TURNER

Moderately

As I stray'd from my cot— at the close of the day, 'Mid the
As the hart on the moun-tain my lov-er was brave, So no-

rav-ish-ing beau-ties of June, 'Neath a jess-a-mine shade, I es-
ble and man-ly and clev-er,— So— kind and sin-cere, And he

pied a fair maid, And she plain-tive-ly sighed to the moon!
loved me full dear, Oh, my Ed-win, his e-qual was nev-er!

Refrain

Roll— On, Sil-ver Moon, Guide the trav-'ler his way, While the

night-in-gale's song is in tune;— I— nev-er, nev-er more with my

true love will stray— by thy soft— sil-ver beams, gen-tle moon.

Words by
HOWARD JOHNSON

Andantino
(Starlight and Sunshine)
Mixed Voices

Music by
EDWIN H. LEMARE

Star- light and sun - shine— Will al -ways re - mind me of

you _____ Your eyes are star - light ___ Your

of _ you.

smile is the sun - shine too. _____ Night - time or

day-time — You seem to be al -ways in view _____ Star -
(in view)

light and sun - shine ___ re - mind me ___ of you. ___

Ben Bolt

THOMAS DUNN ENGLISH

NELSON KNEASS

1. Oh! don't you re-mem-ber_ sweet Al-ice, Ben Bolt, Sweet Al-ice whose hair was so
2. Un-der the hick-o-ry tree, Ben Bolt, Which stood at the foot of the
3. There is change in the things I loved, Ben Bolt, They have chang'd from the old to the

brown, Who wept with de-light when you gave her a smile, And_
hill, To - geth - er we've lain in the noon - day shade, And_
new; But I feel in the depths of my spir - it the truth, There

trem-bled with fear_ at your frown? In the old church yard, in the
lis - tened to Ap - ple-ton's mill. The_ mill wheel_ has fal-len to
nev - er was change in_ you. Twelve months twen - ty_ have_

val-ley, Ben Bolt, In a cor-ner ob-scure and a - lone, They have fit-ted a slab of the
pie-ces, Ben Bolt, The_ raf-ters have turn-bled in, And a qui-et that crawls round the
past, Ben Bolt, Since first we were friends yet I hail Thy_ pres-ence a bless-ing, thy

gran - ite so gray, And sweet Al - ice lies un - der the stone, They have
walls as you gaze, Has_ fol-lowed the old - en_ din, And a
friend-ship a truth, Ben_ Bolt of the salt - sea_ gale, Thy_

ad libitum

fit - ted a slab of the gran-ite so gray, And sweet Al-ice lies un - der the stone.
qui - et that crawls round the walls as you gaze, Has_ fol-lowed the old - en_ din.
pres-ence a bless-ing thy friend-ship a truth, Ben_ Bolt of the salt-sea_ gale!

Juanita

Mrs. CAROLINE NORTON

Soft o'er the foun - tain, Lin - g'ring falls the south - ern moon;
When in thy dream - ing Moons like these shall shine a - gain,

Far o'er the moun - tain, Breaks the day too soon!
And day - light beam - ing, Prove thy dreams are vain,

In thy dark eyes' splen - dor, Where the warm light loves to dwell,
Wilt thou not, re - lent - ing, For thine ab - sent lov - er sigh?

Wea - ry looks, yet ten - der, Speak their fond fare - well.
In thy heart con - sent - ing To a prayer gone by.

Refrain

Ni - ta! Jua - ni - ta! Ask thy soul if we should part!
Ni - ta! Jua - ni - ta! Let me lin - ger by thy side!

Ni - ta! Jua - ni - ta! Lean thou on my heart.
Ni - ta! Jua - ni - ta! Be my own Fair Bride.

Flow Gently, Sweet Afton

ROBERT BURNS

J. E. SPILMAN

Without dragging

1. Flow Gen-tly, Sweet Af-ton, a-mong thy green braes; Flow gen-tly, I'll
2. How loft-y sweet Af-ton, thy neigh-bor-ing hills; Far marked with the
3. Thy crys-tal stream, Af-ton, how love-ly it glides, And winds by the

sing thee a song in thy praise; My Ma-ry's a-sleep by thy mur-mur-ing
cours-es of clear-wind-ing rills! There dai-ly I-wan-der as morn ris-es
cot where my Ma-ry re-sides! How wan-ton thy-wa-ters her snow-y feet

stream, Flow Gen-tly, Sweet Af-ton, dis-turb not her dream, Thou
high, My flocks and my Ma-ry's sweet cot in my eye. How
lave, As gath-'ring sweet flow-'rets, she stems thy clear wave! Flow

stock-dove, whose ech-o re-sounds from the hill, Ye-wild whist-ling
pleas-ant thy-banks and green val-leys be-low, Where wild in the
Gen-tly, Sweet Af-ton, a-mong thy green braes, Flow-Gen-tly, Sweet

black-birds in yon-thorn-y-dell, Thou green-crest-ed-lap-wing, thy
wood-lands the prim-ros-es-blow, There oft as mild-eve-ning creeps
riv-er, the theme of my-lays; My Ma-ry's a-sleep by thy

scream-ing for-bear. I charge you, dis-turb not my slum-ber-ing fair.
o-ver the lea, The sweet-scent-ed birk shades my Ma-ry and me.
mur-mur-ing stream, Flow Gen-tly, Sweet Af-ton, dis-turb not her dream.

Drink To Me Only With Thine Eyes

BEN JONSON   OLD ENGLISH

Slowly, with expression

1. Drink To Me On - ly With Thine Eyes, And I will pledge with mine
2. I sent thee late a ro - sy wreath, Not so much hon -'ring thee

Or leave a kiss with - in the cup, And I'll not ask for wine; The
As giv - ing it a hope that there It could not with-ered be; But

thirst that from the soul doth rise, Doth ask a drink di - vine;
thou there-on did'st on - ly breathe, And send'st it back to me,

rit.

But might I of Jove's nec - tar sup I would not change for thine.
Since when it grows and smells I swear, Not of it-self but thee.

Dear Evelina

Waltz tempo

1. Way down in the mead-ow where the lil - y first blows, Where the wind from the
2. She's fair like a rose, like a lamb she is meek, And she nev - er was

moun-tains ne'er ruf - fles the rose; Lives fond Ev - e - li - na, the
known to put paint on her cheek; In the most grace-ful curls hangs her

sweet lit - tle dove, The_ pride of the val-ley, the girl that I love.
ra- ven black hair, And she nev - er re - quires per - fum-er - y there.

Refrain

Dear Ev - e - li - na, sweet Ev - e - li - na, My love for

thee shall nev - er, nev-er die; nev - er, nev-er die.
nev - er, nev-er die;

nev - er die;

All Through The Night

H. BOULTON   OLD WELSH AIR

Softly

1. Sleep, my child, and peace at-tend thee All Thro' The Night; Guar-dian an-gels
2. While the moon her watch is keep-ing All Thro' The Night; While the wea-ry

God will send thee All Thro' The Night, Soft the drow-sy hours are creep-ing,
world is sleep-ing All Thro' The Night, O'er thy spir- it gen - tly steal-ing,

Hill and vale in slum-ber steep-ing, I my lov-ing vig-il keep-ing All Thro' The Night.
Vis-ions of de-light re - veal-ing, Breathes a pure and ho-ly feel-ing All Thro' The Night.

Still As The Night

CARL BOHM

Whispering Hope

ALICE HAWTHORNE

joice   *rall.*

joice Ah! ___ Whis - per-ing Hope, ___ Oh, how wel -
joice   Oh, how

joice Whis-per - ing Hope, ___ Oh, how wel -

voice. ___   *rall.*

- come thy voice ⎫ thy voice Mak - ing my heart ___ in its
wel-come thy voice ⎭   in its

come thy voice ___   in its

sor - row re - ⌜1.⌝   ⌜2.⌝ *p*

sor - row re - joice. ___   joice. Ah! re - joice. ___
sor - row re -

sor - row re -

The Quilting Party

Andante

1. In the sky the bright stars glit - tered, _ On the bank the pale moon shone;⎫
2. On my arm a soft hand rest - ed, _ Rest - ed light as o - cean foam;⎭

Fine

And 'twas from Aunt Din-ah's quilt-ing par-ty, I was see-ing Nel-lie home.

D.S. And 'twas from Aunt Din-ah's quilt-ing par-ty I was see-ing Nel-lie home.

D.S.

I was see-ing Nel-lie home, ___ I was see-ing Nel-lie home;

John Peel

Male Voices

OLD ENGLISH MELODY

D' ye ken John Peel with his coat so gay, D' ye
D' ye ken John Peel with his coat so gay, He

ken John Peel at the break of the day, D' ye ken John Peel when he's
lived at Trout-beck Once on a day; But now he's gone far a-

far, far a-way, With his hounds and his horn in the morn-ing.
way, far a-way, We shall ne'er hear his voice in the morn-ing.

Ta - ra! Ta - ra! Ta - ra!

T'was the sound of his horn brought me from my bed And the cry of his hounds which he

Tan-ta-ra! Tan-ta-ra! Tan-ta-ra!

Ta ra! Peel's

oft-times led; Peel's "view-hal-loo" would wak-en the dead, Or the

Tan-ta-ra! Peel's

1.

fox from his lair in the morn-ing.

D.C.

2. rall.

fox from his lair, in the morn-ing.

The Low-Backed Car

SAMUEL LOVER

OLD IRISH AIR

Brightly

1. When first I saw sweet Peg-gy, 'Twas on a mar-ket day, A lowback'd car she
2. In bat-tle's wild com-mo-tion, The proud and might-y Mars, With hos-tile scythes, de-
3. Sweet Peg-gy round her car, sir, Has strings of ducks and geese, But the scores of hearts she

drove, and sat Up-on a truss of hay; But when that hay was bloom-ing grass, And
mands his tithes Of death, in war-like cars; While Peg-gy peace-ful god-dess, Has
slaugh-ters By far out-num-ber these, While she a-mong her poul-try sits, Just

deck'd with flow'rs of spring, No flow'r was there that would compare With the bloom-ing girl I
darts in her bright eye, That knock men down in the mar-ket town As right and left they
like a tur-tle dove, Well worth the cage, I do en-gage Of the bloom-ing God of

sing, As she sat in The Low Back'd Car;— The man at the turn-pike bar Nev-er
fly, While she sits in her low back'd car;—Than bat-tles more dan-gerous far For the
Love! While she sits in her low back'd car;— The lov-ers come near and far And

rall.   a tempo   rall.

ask'd for the toll, But just rubb'd his auld poll, And look'd af-ter The Low Back'd Car.
doc-tor's art Can-not cure the heart, That is hit from The Low Back'd Car.
en-vy the chick-en That Peg-gy is pickin', As she sits in The Low Back'd Car.

I'll Take You Home Again, Kathleen

Words and Music by
THOMAS P. WESTENDORF

Slow, with expression

1. I'll Take You Home A-gain, Kath-leen, dear Kath-leen. A-cross the o-cean wild and
2. I know you love me, Kath-leen, dear, Kath-leen dear, Your heart was ev-er fond and

wide, To where your heart has ev-er been, ev-er been, Since first you were my bon-nie
true; I al-ways feel when you are near, you are near, That life holds noth-ing dear, but

bride, bon-nie bride. The ro-ses all have left your cheek, have left your cheek I've
you, dear, but you. The smiles that once you gave to me, you gave to me, I

watched them fade a-way and die; — Your voice is sad when e'er you speak, And
scarce-ly ev-er see them now; — Tho' man-y man-y times I see, — A

Chorus

tears be-dim your lov-ing eyes. —
dark-'ning shad-ow on your brow. —
Oh! I will take you back a-

gain, back a-gain, To where your heart will feel no pain, And when the fields are fresh and

rall.

green,————— I'll take you to your home a - gain, Dear Kath-leen.
Fresh and green,

The Vacant Chair

Slowly

GEORGE F. ROOT

1. We shall meet, but we shall miss him, There will be one va - cant
2. At our fire-side, sad and lone-ly, Oft - en will the bo - som
3. True, they tell us wreaths of glo - ry Ev - er - more will deck his

D.C. We shall meet, but we shall miss him, There will be one va - cant

chair; We shall lin - ger to ca - ress him, When we breathe our ev-'ning pray'r.
swell; At re - mem-brance of the sto - ry How our no - ble Wil-lie fell;
brow, But this sooth's the an-guish on - ly Sweep-ing o'er our heart-strings now.

Fine

chair; We shall lin - ger to ca - ress him, When we breathe our ev-'ning pray'r.

When a year a - go we gath-er'd, Joy was in his mild blue eye, But a
How he strove to bear our ban-ner Thro' the thick-est of the fight, And up-
Sleep to - day, O ear-ly fall-en, In thy green and nar-row bed, Dir-ges

gold - en cord is sev - ered, And our hopes in ru - in lie.
hold our coun-try's hon - or, In the strength of man-hood's might.
from the pine and cy - press Min - gle with the tears we shed.

D.C.

English Lyric by
HOWARD JOHNSON

Wiegenlied
Cradle Song

Music by
JOHANNES BRAHMS

Dear goodnight, yes goodnight Mis-ter Sand-man is call-ing Sail a - way to Blank-et Bay And re-turn at break of day Close your eyes,_ lul - la - bys soon will ban-ish all harms With the bright morn-ing light You'll be back in my arms.

Sally In Our Alley

HENRY CUREY

Moderately

1. Of all the girls that are so smart, There's none like pret-ty Sal-ly; She is the dar-ling of my heart And lives in our al - ley; There
2. Of all the days with-in the week,_ I dear-ly love but one day; And that's the day that comes be - twixt The Sat-ur-day and Mon-day; Oh,
3. My mas-ter and the neigh-bors all,_ Make game of me and Sal-ly; And but for her I'd rath-er be_ A slave, and row a gal-ley; But

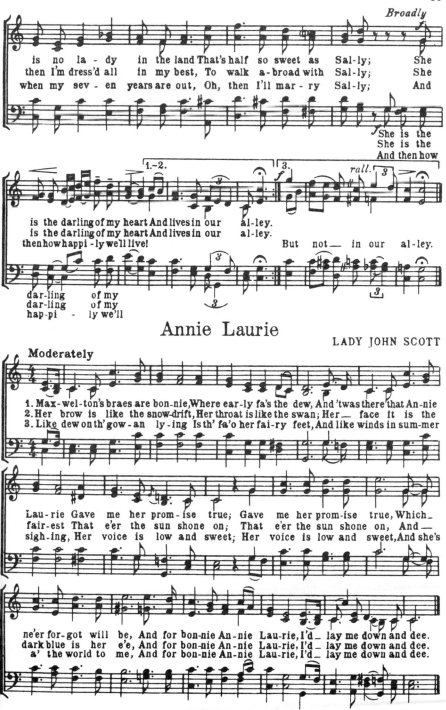

Broadly

is no la - dy in the land That's half so sweet as Sal-ly; She
then I'm dress'd all in my best, To walk a-broad with Sal-ly; She
when my sev - en years are out, Oh, then I'll mar - ry Sal-ly; And

She is the
She is the
And then how

1.-2.   3.   rall.

is the darling of my heart And lives in our al-ley.
is the darling of my heart And lives in our al-ley.
then how happi - ly we'll live!   But not_ in our al-ley.

dar-ling of my
dar-ling of my
hap-pi - ly we'll

Annie Laurie

LADY JOHN SCOTT

Moderately

1. Max-wel-ton's braes are bon-nie, Where ear-ly fa's the dew, And 'twas there that An-nie
2. Her brow is like the snow-drift, Her throat is like the swan; Her_ face it is the
3. Like dew on th' gow-an ly-ing Is th' fa'o her fai-ry feet, And like winds in sum-mer

Lau-rie Gave me her prom-ise true; Gave me her prom-ise true, Which_
fair-est That e'er the sun shone on; That e'er the sun shone on, And _
sigh-ing, Her voice is low and sweet; Her voice is low and sweet, And she's

ne'er for-got will be, And for bon-nie An-nie Lau-rie, I'd_ lay me down and dee.
dark blue is her e'e, And for bon-nie An-nie Lau-rie, I'd _ lay me down and dee.
a' the world to me, And for bon-nie An-nie Lau-rie, I'd_ lay me down and dee.

Last Night

HALFDAN KJERULK

Moderately, flowing tempo

Last night the night-in-gale woke me, Last night when all was still ____ It
I think of you in the day - time, I dream of you by night ____ I

sang in the gold - en moon - light, From out ____ the wood-land hill, I
wake _ and would you were here, love, And tears ____ are blind-ing my sight. I

o-pen'd my win-dow so _ gent - ly, I look'd on the dream-ing dew, ____ And
hear a low breath in the _ lime tree, The wind _ is float-ing thru, ____ And

rit.

oh! _ the bird, my dar-ling, Was sing - ing, sing-ing of _ you, of you. ____
oh! _ the night, my dar-ling, Is sigh - ing, sigh-ing for _ you, for you. ____

rit.

When Love Is Kind

THOMAS MOORE   OLD MELODY

Gracefully

1. When Love Is Kind, ___ cheer - ful and free, ___
2. If love can sigh, ___ for one a - lone, ___
3. Love must in short, ___ keep fond and true, ___

Love's sure to find ___ wel - come from me;
Well pleased am I ___ to be that one;
Thru good re - port, ___ and e - vil too;

to find wel - come from me;
to be ___ that one;
and ___ e - vil too;

But when love brings ___ heart-ache and pang, ___ Tears and such things, -
But should I see ___ love giv'n to rove, ___ To two, or three, ___
Else here I swear, ___ young love may go, ___ For aught I care, ___

(Solo or unison)
Ah!

1. 2.   3.

love may go hang.
then good - bye love.   to Je - ri - cho!   to

(p)

rall.

ha! ha! ha! To Je - ri - cho!

Je - ri - cho, Je - ri - cho,   Je - ri - cho!

Who Is Sylvia

SHAKESPEARE

FRANZ SCHUBERT

Moderate, well marked

1. Who Is Syl - via? What _ is she, That all our swains com -
2. Is she kind, as she _ is fair? For beau - ty lives with
3. Then to Syl - via let _ us sing, That Syl - via is ex -

mend her? Ho - ly, fair, _ and wise is she; _ The
kind - ness; To her eyes _ love doth re - pair, _ To
cel - ling; She ex - cells _ each mor - tal thing, _ Up -

heav'ns such grace did lend _ her; _ That a - dor - ed _
help him of his - blind - ness; _ And, be - ing help'd _ in -
on the dull earth dwell - ing; _ To her gar - lands _

might _
its _
us _

lend her,
blind - ness;
dwell - ing;

she might be, _ That a - dor - ed she might be.
hab - its there, And be - ing help'd in - hab - its there.
let us bring, _ To her gar - lands let us bring.

When The Corn Is Waving

CHARLES BLAMPHIN

Slowly

1. When The Corn Is Wav - ing, An - nie dear, Oh, meet me by the
2. When The Corn Is Wav - ing, An - nie dear, Our tales of love we'll

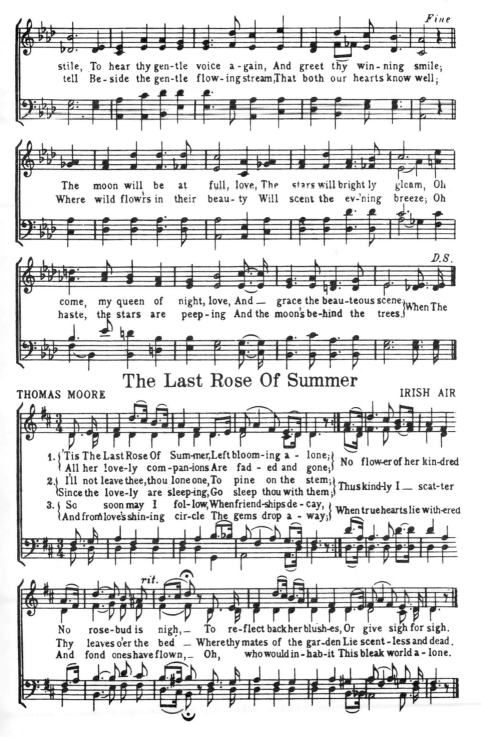

stile, To hear thy gen-tle voice a-gain, And greet thy win-ning smile;
tell Be-side the gen-tle flow-ing stream,That both our hearts know well;

Fine

The moon will be at full, love, The stars will bright ly gleam, Oh
Where wild flow'rs in their beau-ty Will scent the ev-'ning breeze; Oh

D.S.

come, my queen of night, love, And — grace the beau-teous scene. When The
haste, the stars are peep-ing And the moon's be-hind the trees.

The Last Rose Of Summer

THOMAS MOORE   IRISH AIR

1. 'Tis The Last Rose Of Sum-mer, Left bloom-ing a - lone;
   All her love-ly com-pan-ions Are fad - ed and gone;
   No flow-er of her kin-dred

2. I'll not leave thee, thou lone one, To pine on the stem;
   Since the love-ly are sleep-ing, Go sleep thou with them;
   Thus kind-ly I — scat-ter

3. So soon may I fol-low, When friend-ships de - cay,
   And from love's shin-ing cir-cle The gems drop a - way;
   When true hearts lie with-ered

rit.

No rose-bud is nigh, — To re-flect back her blush-es, Or give sigh for sigh.
Thy leaves o'er the bed — Where thy mates of the gar-den Lie scent-less and dead.
And fond ones have flown, — Oh, who would in-hab-it This bleak world a - lone.

Twickenham Ferry

THEO. MARZIALS

Brightly

1. O hoi-ye ho, Ho-ye-ho Who's for the fer-ry The bri-ar's in bud,—The
2. O hoi-ye ho, Ho-ye-ho I'm for the fer-ry The bri-ar's in bud,—The

sun go-ing down, And I'll row ye so quick and I'll row ye so stea-dy, And
sun go-ing down, And it's late as it is, and I have-n't a pen-ny, And

'tis but a pen-ny to Twick-en-ham Town. The— Fer- ry-man's slim and the
how shall I get me to Twick-en-ham Town. She'd a rose in her bon-net, and

Fer-ry-man's young, And he's just a soft twang in the turn of his tongue, And he's
Oh! she looked sweet, As the lit-tle pink flow-er that grows in the wheat, With her

fresh as a pip-pin and brown as a ber-ry, And 'tis but a pen-ny to
cheeks like a rose and her lips like a cher-ry, And

1.

2.   rall.   fa tempo

Twick-en-ham Town.
sure and you're wel-come, To   Twick-en-ham Town.

Londonderry Air

Slow *(with expression)*

OLD IRISH MELODY

Would God I were the ten-der ap-ple blos-som—That floats and

falls from off the twist-ed bough,— To lie and faint with-in your silk-en

poco rit. *a tempo*

bo-som, With-in your silk-en bo-som, As that does now!— Or would I

mf *cresc.* pluck me,

were a lit-tle bur-nished ap-ple— For you to pluck me, glid-ing by so

shade your

ff

cold,— While sun and shade your robe of lawn will

shade your

p *rall.*

dap-ple,— Your robe of lawn And— your hair's spun gold.—

Kathleen Mavourneen

MRS. JULIA CRAWFORD

FREDERICK CROUCH

1. Kath-leen Ma-vour-neen! The grey dawn is break-ing The horn of the hunt-er — is — heard — on the hill, The lark from her light wing the bright dew is shak - ing, — Kath-leen Ma-vour-neen! What, slum-b'ring still? Oh! hast thou for - got - ten how soon we must sev- er? Oh! hast thou for - got-ten this day we must part? years, and it may be for - ev- er; Oh! why — art thou si - lent, thou

2. Kath-leen Ma-vour-neen! A - wake from thy slum-bers The blue moun-tains glow in — the — sun's — gold-en light, Ah! where is the spell that once hung on thy num - bers, A - rise in thy beau-ty thou star of my night! Ma-vour-neen, Ma- vour-neen, my sad tears are fall-ing, To think that from E - rin and thee I must part.

It may be for

* Melody in Alto voice should predominate.

voice of my heart? It may— be for years and it may be for-

ev-er; Then why— art thou si-lent, Kath-leen Ma-vour-neen?

Songs My Mother Taught Me

ANTON DVÔRÁK

Slowly, with motion

Songs My Moth-er Taught— Me, In the days long van-ished,

Sel-dom from her eye-lids, Where the tear-drops ban-ished.

Now I teach my chil-dren, Each mel-o-dious mea-sure.

Oft the tears are flow-ing, Oft they flow— from my mem-ry's trea-sure.—

flow-ing

The Rose Of Tralee

Words by
C. MORDAUNT SPENCER

Music by
CHARLES W. GLOVER

The pale moon was ris-ing a-bove the green moun-tain, The sun was de-
The cool shade of eve-ning their man-tle were spread-ing, And Ma-ry all

clin-ing be-neath the blue sea, When I strayed with my love to the
smil-ing was list-'ning to me, The— moon thro' the val-ley, her

pure crys-tal foun-tain That stands in the beau-ti-ful vale of Tra-
pale rays was shed-ding, When I won the heart of The Rose Of Tra-

lee; She was love-ly and fair as the rose of_ the sum-mer, Yet
lee; Though love-ly and fair as the rose of_ the sum-mer,

'twas not her beau-ty a-lone that won me, Oh, no! 'twas the

truth in her eye ev-er dawn-ing, That made me love Ma-ry, The

When You And I Were Young, Maggie

GEORGE W. JOHNSON

J.A.BUTTERFIELD

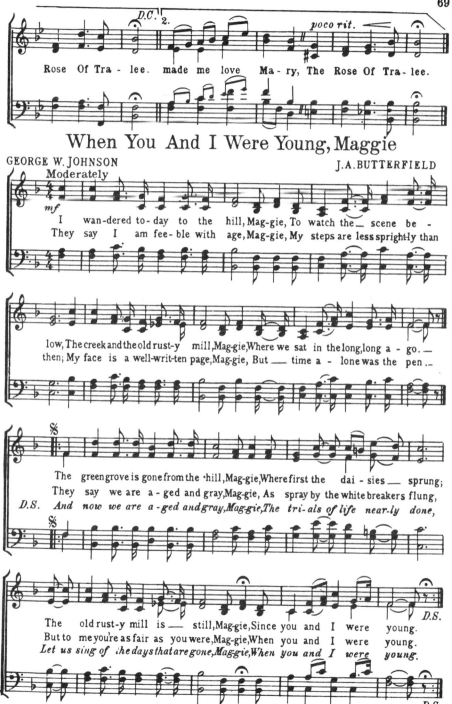

70

HOWARD JOHNSON

Dark Eyes

A. SALAMI

Dear Dark Eyes that shine, I once thought were mine Just for
Auld Lang Syne, please come back some time To your bal - co - ny,
and look down at me Bring back par - a - dise, Dear Dark Eyes.

Copyright © 1932 (Renewed 1960) LEO FEIST, INC.

HOWARD JOHNSON

Viennese Refrain

An old re - frain is al - ways haunt - ing me I heard in child-hood days at Moth-er's
knee There in the can-dle light so ten-der - ly She'd sing a song that lives in mem-o -
ry A strain of hap-pi-ness that dear-er grows A hymn of love that just a Moth-er

knows And as my tir-ed eyes be-gan to close At peace with all the world, I'd find re - pose.

Refrain

Gone are those hap-py days so Hea-ven sent If I could

mf

live them o'er I'd be con - tent Now ev-'ry night when shad-ows cov-er

me I miss that old re-frain of mem - o - ry.

poco rit.

Passing By

EDWARD PURCELL

Slowly *(softly)*

There is a la-dy sweet and kind, Was nev-er face so pleas'd my mind;
Her ges-ture, mo-tion and her smiles, Her wit, her voice my heart be - guiles,

I did but see her Pass-ing By, And yet I love her, 'till I die.
Be-guiles my heart, I know not why, And yet I love her, 'till I die.

J. MACKLYN MESKILL

Cielito Lindo
(Beautiful Heaven)

C. FERNANDEZ

Santa Lucia

Ciribiribee

HOWARD JOHNSON
Waltz tempo

A. PESTALOZZA

Funiculi - Funiculà
A Happy Heart

HOWARD JOHNSON

LUIGI DENZA

March tempo

Chorus (*March tempo*)

Join' the chor-us, now's the time to start__ Sing the chor-us

with a hap-py heart Tra, la, la, la, la, la, la, la, la, la, la, do your lit-tle part

Let the ech-o ring and sing it with A Hap-py Heart. with A Hap-py Heart.

There's Music In The Air

Moderately fast   GEORGE F. ROOT

1. There's Mu-sic In The Air When the in-fant morn is nigh, And faint its blush is seen
2. There's Mu-sic In The Air When the noon-tide's sul-try beam Re-flects a gold-en .light
3. There's Mu-sic In The Air When the twi-light's gen-tle sigh Is lost on eve-ning's breast,

On the bright and laugh-ing sky. Many a harp's ec-stat-ic sound, With its thrill of
On the dis-tant moun-tain stream. When be-neath some grate-ful shade, Sor-row's ach-ing
As its pen-sive beau-ties die. Then, oh, then the loved ones gone Wake the pure ce-

joy pro-found, While we list, en-chant-ed there, To the mu-sic in the air.
head is laid, Sweet-ly to the spir-it there, Comes the mu-sic in the air.
les-tial song, An-gel voi-ces greet us there, In the mu-sic in the air.

RAYMOND KLAGES

Down De Road

ANTON DVŎRÁK

Very slow

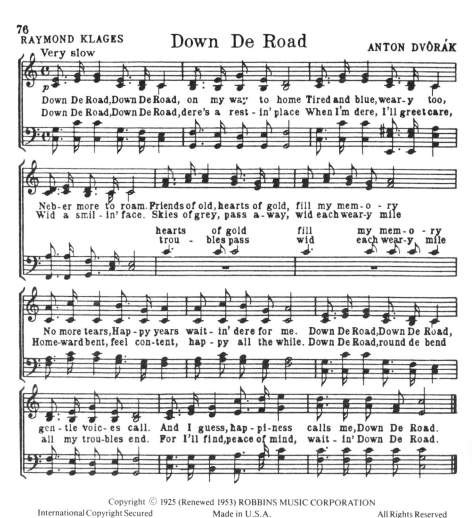

Down De Road, Down De Road, on my way to home Tired and blue, wear-y too,
Down De Road, Down De Road, dere's a rest-in' place When I'm dere, I'll greet care,

Neb-er more to roam. Friends of old, hearts of gold, fill my mem-o-ry
Wid a smil-in' face. Skies of grey, pass a-way, wid each wear-y mile

hearts of gold fill my mem-o-ry
trou - bles pass wid each wear-y mile

No more tears, Hap-py years wait-in' dere for me. Down De Road, Down De Road,
Home-ward bent, feel con-tent, hap-py all the while. Down De Road, round de bend

gen-tle voic-es call. And I guess, hap-pi-ness calls me, Down De Road.
all my trou-bles end. For I'll find, peace of mind, wait-in' Down De Road.

HOWARD JOHNSON

Liebestraum

FRANZ LISZT

Moderato (slowly with expression)

My Dream Of Love will lin-ger on for - ev - er al-tho' we are far a-

part My Dream Of Love, will lin-ger tho' I know It

far a-part

The Soldier's Farewell

JOHANNA KINKEL

1. How can I bear to leave thee? One part-ing kiss I give thee; And
2. Ne'er more may I be-hold thee, Or to this heart en-fold thee; With

then what-e'er be - falls me, I go where hon - or calls me,
guns and pen-nons glanc-ing, I see the foe ad - vanc-ing,

Fare-well, fare-well, my own true love; Fare-well, fare - well, my own true love.

My Blue Danube
(Blue Danube)

HOWARD JOHNSON

JOHANN STRAUSS

Oh Marie
Maria, Mari!

HOWARD JOHNSON

E. DI CAPUA

cresc. — *f* — *a tempo*

-rie, ___ Oh Ma - rie, ___ I can't seem to go on dear with - out you ___
-ri - a, Ma - ri! ___ Quan-ta suon-no che per-do pe - te!

poco dim.

You're meant. for me ___ Oh Ma - rie ___ Oh Ma - rie, ___
Fam - m'ad - dur - mi ___ Oj Ma - ri ___ Oj Ma - ri!

Oh, My Darling Clementine

Moderately

P. MONTROSE

1. In a cav - ern, in a can - yon, Ex - ca - vat - ing for a
2. Light she was and like a fai - ry, And her shoes were num - ber
3. Drove she duck-lings to the wat - er, Ev - 'ry morn - ing just at
4. Ru - by lips a - bove the wat - er, Blow - ing bub - bles soft and

mine, Dwelt a min - er, for - ty nin - er, And his daugh-ter Cle-men - tine.
nine; Her - ring box - es, with - out top - ses San - dals were for Cle-men - tine.
nine, Hit her foot a-gainst a splin - ter, Fell in - to the foam-ing brine.
fine; A - las for me! I was no swim-mer, So I lost my Cle-men - tine.

Refrain

Oh my dar - ling, Oh my dar - ling, Oh My Dar-ling Cle-men - tine, You are

f

lost and gone for - ev - er, Dred - ful sor - ry, Cle - men - tine.

The Voice In The Old Village Choir

GUS KAHN

HARRY WOODS

Thine Eyes So Blue And Tender

E. LASSEN

spell, ____ Such dreams and thoughts come to ____ me,
old, ____ Thou'rt wind - ing chains a - bout ____ me,

Which e'en I dare not tell. ____ With eyes so blue and
Which ne'er will lose their hold With hair so soft and

dream - ing, That haunt me ev - 'ry - where, ____ A
gold' - en, Heart pure and all mine own, ____ Thou'lt

fair blue sea ____ of fan - cies Takes from my heart all care. ____
ev - er hold ____ me cap - tive Un - to the si - lent tomb. ____

Stars Of The Summer Night

LONGFELLOW   L.B.WOODBURY

1. Stars Of The Sum-mer Night, Far in yon az - ure deep, Hide, hide your
2. Moon of the sum-mer night, Far down yon west-ern steeps, Sink, sink in
3. Dreams of the sum-mer night, Tell her, her lov - er keeps Watch, while, in

gold - en light, }
sil - ver light, } She sleeps, my la - dy sleeps, She sleeps, She sleeps, my la-dy sleeps.
slum-ber light, }

Rocked In The Cradle Of The Deep

EMMA WILLARD

JOSEPH P. KNIGHT

1. Rocked In The Cra-dle Of The Deep, I lay me down in peace to sleep; Se-
2. And such the trust that still were mine, Tho'storm-y winds sweep o'er the brine, Or

cure I rest up-on the wave, For Thou, O Lord, hast pow'r to save. I
though the tem-pest's fier-y breath Rouse me from sleep to wreck and death, In

know Thou wilt not slight my call, For Thou dost mark the spar-row's fall; And
o-cean cave still safe with Thee, The germ of im-mor-tal-i-ty;

calm and peace-ful is my sleep, Rocked In The Cra-dle Of The Deep; And calm and peaceful is my

sleep, Rocked In The Cra-dle Of The Deep. Rocked In The Cra-dle Of The Deep.

Rocked In The Cradle Of The Deep.

Over The Summer Sea

G. VERDI

Brightly

1. O-ver The Sum-mer Sea, With light hearts gay and free,
2. List, to my roun-de-lay As we glide on our way;

Join'd by glad min-strel-sy, Gai-ly we're roam-ing; Swift flows the
Ne'er will my love de-cay, Ne'er will I leave thee, While o'er the

rip-pling tide; Light-ly the zeph-yrs glide; Round us, on ev-'ry side,
wa-ters deep; Now our oars gai-ly sweep; True in the time they keep,

Bright crests are foam - ing. Fond hearts en - twin - ing,
What ___ can grieve___ thee?

Cease all re - pin-ing; Near us is shin-ing Beau - ty's bright smile.

Now The Day Is Over

SABINE BARING-GOULD   JOSEPH BARNBY

1. Now The Day Is O - ver, Night is draw - ing nigh,
2. Je - sus, give the wea - ry Calm and sweet re - pose,
3. When the morn-ing wak - ens, Then may we a - rise

Shad - ows of the ev' - ning Steal a - cross the sky.
With Thy tend-'rest bless - ing, May our eye - lids close.
Pure and fresh and sin - less In Thy ho - ly eyes.

Go To Sleep, Lena Darling

J.K. EMMET

Slowly

1. Close your eyes, Le - na, my dar - ling, While I sing your lul - la-
2. Bright be de morn - ing, my dar - ling, Ven you ope your eyes;

Close your eyes, Le - na, dar - ling
Bright de morn - ing, my dar - ling

rall.   a tempo

by; Fear thou no dan - ger, Le - na, Move not, dear Le - na, my dar - ling,
Sun-beams glow all 'round you, Le - na, Peace be with thee, love, my dar - ling,

Move not
Peace with

rall.

For your broo - der watch - es near you Le - na dear. An - gels guide thee,
Blue and cloud - less be the sky for Le - na dear. Birds sing their bright

Le - na dear, my dar - ling, Noth - ing e - vil can come near;
songs for thee, my dar - ling, Full of sweet - est mel - o - dy;

Bright - est flow - ers blow for thee, Dar - ling sis - ter, dear to me.
An - gels ev - er hov - er near, Dar - ling sis - ter, dear to me.

Refrain

Go to sleep, Go to sleep my ba - by, my ba - by, my ba - by.

Go to sleep my ba - by, ba - by, oh bye! Go to Sleep, Le-na,_ Sleep.
(sleep)

Woodman, Spare That Tree

HENRY RUSSELL

Moderate

1. Wood-man, Spare That Tree!_ Touch not a sin - gle bough; In
2. That old fa - mil - iar tree!_ Its glo - ry and re - nown, Are

youth it shel - tered me, And I'll pro - tect it now; 'Twas
spread o'er land and sea, And wouldst thou hew it down? Wood-

my fore-fa - ther's hand, That placed it near his cot, There,
man, for - bear thy stroke! Cut not its earth-bound ties, Oh!

Wood - man, let it stand, Thy __ axe shall harm it not!
spare that a - ged oak, Now __ tow'r - ing to the skies.

A Capital Ship

Male Voices

CHARLES E. CARRYL

Well marked
Solo or unison

1. A Cap-i-tal Ship for an o - cean trip Was the Wal-lop-ing__ Win - dow
2. The bo'-swan's mate was__ ve - ry se - date, Yet__ fond__ of a-muse-ment,
3. The Cap -tain sat on the Com-mo-dore's hat, And__ dined__ in a roy - al

Blind! No wind that blew dis - mayed__ her crew, Or __
too; He played hop - scotch with the star - board watch, While the
way, Off toast - ed pigs and__ pick-les and figs And __

trou-bled the__ Cap' - tain's mind; The man__ at the wheel was
Cap - tain he tick-led the crew! And the gun-ner we__ had was ap-
gun-ne-ry__ bread each day. And the cook__ was__ Dutch, and be-

made__ to feel Con - tempt for the wild - est blow - ow - ow,
par - ent-ly mad, For he sat on the aft - er rai - ai - ail,
haved__ as such, For the di - et he gave the crew - ew - ew,

Tho' it
And __
Was a

H'm _____

been in his bunk__ be - low.
teeth of the boom - ing gale!
up with__ su-gar and glue.

H'm _____

oft- en ap-peared, When the gale had cleared, That he'd
fired sa-lutes with the Cap-tain's boots, In the
num-ber of tons of __ hot cross buns Served

Chorus

Then blow, ye winds, heigh - o! A - rov-ing I will go! I'll stay no more on

rit. *Solo or unison*

Eng-land's shore, So let the mu-sic play - ay - ay! I'm off on the morn-ing

(mel.)

train I'll cross the rag-ing main! I'm off to my love With a

1.-2. *Last time Slower* D.C.

box-ing glove, Ten thou-sand miles a - way! thou-sand miles a - way!

The Bell

Key of D

I

The Bell doth toll, its ech - oes roll, I know the sound full

II

well; I love its ring - ing, for it calls to sing - ing With its

III

bim, bim, bim, bome, bell. Bome, bome, bome; bim, bome, bell.

Little Brown Jug

Oh! Susanna

STEPHEN C. FOSTER

see, It rained all night the day I left, The weath-er it was
hill, The buck-wheat cake was in her mouth, The tear was in her

dry, The sun so hot I froze to death; Su-san-na don't you cry.
eye; Say I, I'm com-ing from the South, Su-san-na don't you cry.

Chorus

Oh! Su-san-na Oh! don't you cry for me, I've

come from Al-a-bam-a wid my ban-jo on my knee.

Aloha Oe
(Farewell To Thee)

QUEEN LILIUOKALANI

Chorus
Slowly, with expression

Fare-well To Thee, Fare-well To Thee, Thou charming one who dwells a-mong the

bow-ers, One fond embrace, be-fore I now de-part, Un-til we meet_a-gain. Fare- gain.

Wait For The Wagon

R. B. BUCKLEY

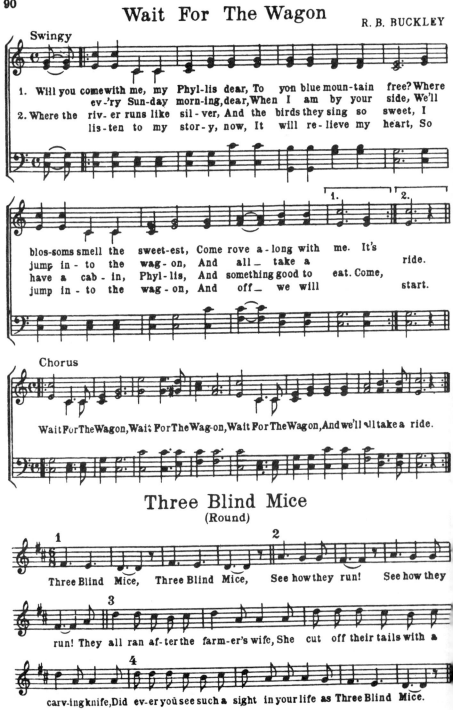

Swingy

1. Will you come with me, my Phyl-lis dear, To yon blue moun-tain free? Where
ev-'ry Sun-day morn-ing, dear, When I am by your side, We'll
2. Where the riv-er runs like sil-ver, And the birds they sing so sweet, I
lis-ten to my stor-y, now, It will re-lieve my heart, So

blos-soms smell the sweet-est, Come rove a-long with me. It's
jump in-to the wag-on, And all __ take a ride.
have a cab-in, Phyl-lis, And something good to eat. Come,
jump in-to the wag-on, And off __ we will start.

Chorus

Wait For The Wagon, Wait For The Wag-on, Wait For The Wagon, And we'll all take a ride.

Three Blind Mice
(Round)

Three Blind Mice, Three Blind Mice, See how they run! See how they
run! They all ran af-ter the farm-er's wife, She cut off their tails with a
carv-ing knife, Did ev-er you see such a sight in your life as Three Blind Mice.

Twinkling Stars Are Laughing, Love

J. P. ORDWAY

Schottisch time

1. Twink-ling Stars Are Laugh-ing, Love, Laugh-ing on you and me;
2. Gold-en beams are shin-ing, love, Shin-ing on you to bless;

and me
to bless

While your bright eyes look in mine, Peep-ing stars they seem to be.
Like the queen of night you fill Dark-est space with love-li-ness.

Trou-bles come and go, love, Bright-est scenes must leave our sight;
Sil-ver stars how bright, love, Moth-er moon in throne-ly might,

rit. *a tempo*

But the star of hope, love, Shines with ra-diant beams to-night.
Gaze on us to bless, love, Pur-est vows here made to-night.

Twink-ling Stars Are Laugh-ing, Love, Laugh-ing on you and me,

While your bright eyes look in mine, Peep-ing stars they seem to be.

Merry Widow Waltz
(Love Remained)

SIDNEY D. MITCHEL

FRANZ LEHAR

Rio Grande
Male Voices

SEA CHANTEY

Were you ev - er in Ri — o Grande?
Where the Port - u - gee girls can be found,
Ri - o, 'way

Ri - o, Oh were you ev - er on that strand? We're
And they are the girls to waltz a - round,

We're bound for, bound for
bound for the Ri - o Grande. Way Ri - o,

We're bound for, bound for
bound for Ri - o rall.
Way Ri - o, Then fare you well, my

bound for Ri - o
pret - ty young girl, We're bound for the Ri - o Grande.

Merrily, Merrily
(Round)

1

2

Mer-ri-ly, mer-ri-ly, greet the morn; Cheer-i-ly, cheer-i-ly sound the horn.

3

4

Hark to the ech-oes, hear them play O'er hill and 'dale, far, far, a-way.

Red River Valley

N. E. PEARSON

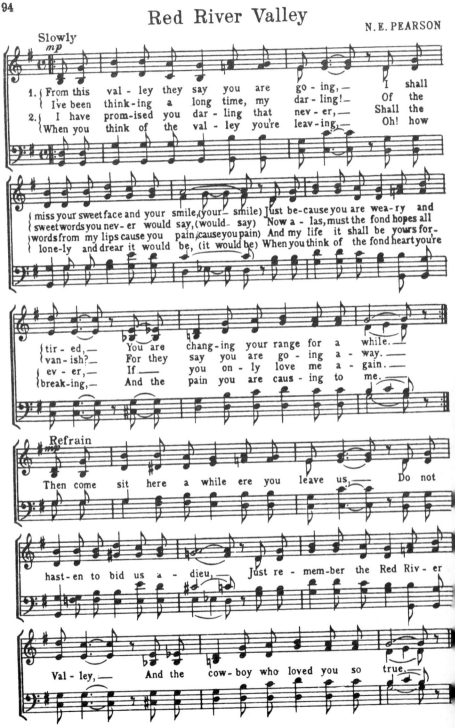

Turkey In The Straw

Paddle Your Own Canoe

M. HOBSON

Slowly

I've trav-ell'd a-bout __ a bit in my time, And of
It's all ver-y well to de-pend on a friend, That __

trou-bles I've seen a few, __ But __ found it bet-ter in
is if you've proved him true. __ But you'll find it bet-ter by

ev-'ry clime To pad-dle my own ca-noe. __
far, in the end To Pad-dle Your Own Ca-noe. __

My wants __ are small __ I care not at all If my
"To bor-row is dear-er by far than to buy," __ A

debts __ are paid when due, __ I drive a-way strife, in the
max-im, tho' old, still true; __ You nev-er will sigh, if you

o-cean of life, While I Pad-dle my own ca-noe. __
on-ly will try To __ Pad-dle Your Own Ca-noe. __

Refrain

Then love your neigh-bor as your-self, As the world you go trav-'ling thru, ____ And nev-er sit down with a tear or a frown, But Pad-dle Your Own Ca-noe. ____

Down In A Coal Mine

Male Voices

Refrain
Moderato

Down In A Coal Mine, un-der-neath the ground, Where a gleam of sun-shine nev-er can be found; Dig-ging dusk-y dia-monds all the sea-son round, Down In A Coal Mine, un-der-neath the ground.

I'se Gwine Back To Dixie

MINSTREL SONG

grow, ___ For I hear de chil-dren call-ing, I see deir sad tears

For

fall-ing, My heart's turned back to Dix-ie, and I must go.

Good-Bye, Liza Jane

MINSTREL SONG

Brightly

I'm goin' a-way to leave you So good-bye, good-bye,

I'm goin' a-way to leave you So Good-bye, Li-za Jane,

I'm goin' a-way to leave you ___ I'm goin' down to Lynch-burg town, If

you get there be-fore I do. It's Good-bye, Li-za Jane.

Whoo-pee Ti Yi Yo
(Git Along, Little Dogies)

COWBOY SONG

Moderato

1. As I was a-walk-ing one morn-ing for pleas-ure, I
2. It's ear-ly in Spring that we round up the do-gies; We

spied a cow-punch-er all rid-ing a-lone, His
mark them and brand them and bob off their tails, We

hat was thrown back and his spurs was a-jing-ling, And
round up our hors-es, load up the chuck-wag-on, And

as he ap-proached he was sing-ing this song:
then throw the do-gies, out on-to the trail.

Refrain

Whoo-pee Ti Yi Yo! Git A-long, Lit-tle Do-gies, It's your mis-for-tune and none of my own. Whoo-pee Ti Yi Yo! — Git A-

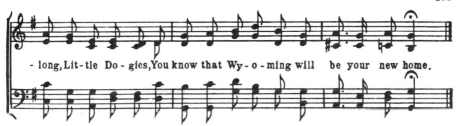

- long, Lit-tle Do - gies, You know that Wy- o -ming will be your new home.

3. Some boys go up the trail for pleasure,
But that's where they gets it most awfully wrong;
For you haven't any idea the trouble they give us
While we go driving them along.

4. Your mother was raised away down in Texas,
Where the jimson weed and sand-burrs grow;
Now we'll fill you up on prickly pear and cholla
Till you are ready for the trail to Idaho.

5. Oh, you'll be soup for Uncle Sam's Injuns;
"It's beef, heap beef," I hear them cry.
Git along, git along, Git Along, Little Dogies,
You'll be beef steers by and by.

Shoo-fly, Don't Bother Me

BILLY REEVES

FRANK CAMPBELL

Lively

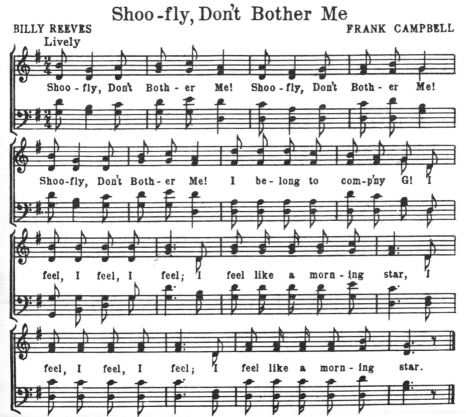

Shoo - fly, Don't Both - er Me! Shoo - fly, Don't Both - er Me!

Shoo-fly, Don't Both-er Me! I be - long to com-p'ny G! I

feel, I feel, I feel; I feel like a morn - ing star, I

feel, I feel, I feel; I feel like a morn - ing star.

The Star-Spangled Banner

FRANCIS SCOTT KEY   (Standard Service Version)   JOHN STAFFORD SMITH

With spirit (♩ = 104)

O— say! can you see by the dawn's ear-ly light, What so proud-ly we hail'd at the
On the shore, dim-ly seen thro' the mists of the deep, Where the foe's haugh-ty host in dread
O— thus be it ev-er when free-men shall stand Be - tween their lov'd homes and the

twi-light's last gleam-ing? Whose broad stripes and bright stars, thro' the per - il-ous fight, O'er the
si-lence re - pos-es, What is that which the breeze, o'er the tow - er-ing steep, As it
war's des-o - la-tion! Blest with vic - t'ry and peace, may the heav'n rescued land Praise the

ram-parts we watched were so gal - lant-ly stream-ing? And the rock-et's red glare, the bomb
fit-ful-ly blows half con-ceals half dis - clos-es? Now it catch-es the gleam of the
Pow'r that hath made and pre-served us a na -tion! Then con-quer we must, when our

Chorus (♩ = 96)

burst-ing in air, Gave proof thro' the night that our flag was still there O— say, does that
morn-ing's first beam, In full glo - ry re-flect-ed now— shines on the stream, 'Tis The Star-spangled
cause it is just, And this be our mot-to: "In — God is our trust!" And The Star-spang led

broaden

Star-span-gled Ban-ner yet wave O'er the land of the free and the home of the brave?
Ban-ner O long may it wave O'er the land of the free and the home of the brave!
Ban-ner in tri-umph shall wave O'er the land of the free and the home of the brave!

Dixie Land

DANIEL EMMET

1. I wish I was in the land of cot-ton, Old times there are not for-got-ten, Look a-
2. Old Mis-sus mar-ry Will "de wea-ber," Wil-lium was a gay de-ceiv-er, Look a-
3. His face was sharp as a butcher's cleaver, But dat did not seem to grieve her, Look a-

way! Look a-way! Look a-way! Dix-ie Land. In— Dix-ie Land where
way! Look a-way! Look a-way! Dix-ie Land. But— when he put his—
way! Look a-way! Look a-way! Dix-ie Land. Old— Mis-sus act-ed the

I was born in,— Ear-ly— on— one frost-y morn-in' Look a-way! Look a-
arm a-round her He smil'd as fierce as a for-ty poun-der Look a-way! Look a-
fool-ish part, And died for a man that broke her heart Look a-way! Look a-

Refrain

way! Look a-way! Dix-ie Land.
way! Look a-way! Dix-ie Land. Then I wish I was in Dix-ie Hoo-ray! Hoo-
way! Look a-way! Dix-ie Land.

ray! In Dix-ie Land, I'll take my stand To live and die in Dix-ie; A-way, A-

way, A-way down south in Dix-ie; A-way, A-way, A-way down south in Dix-ie.

America
My Country 'Tis Of Thee

S.F.SMITH

HENRY CAREY

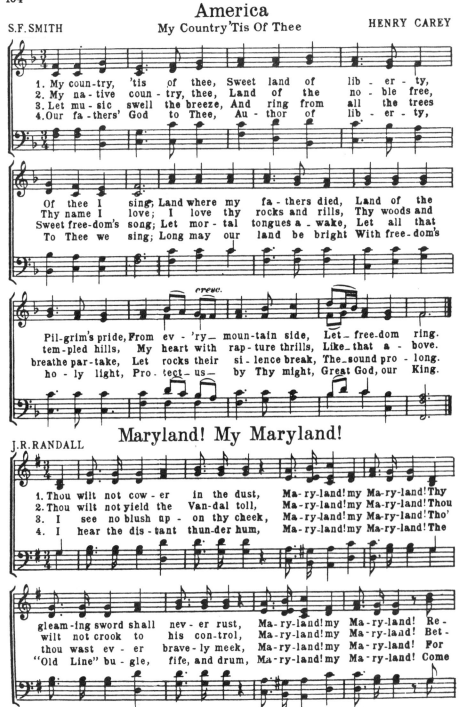

1. My coun-try, 'tis of thee, Sweet land of lib - er - ty,
2. My na - tive coun - try, thee, Land of the no - ble free,
3. Let mu - sic swell the breeze, And ring from all the trees
4. Our fa - thers' God to Thee, Au - thor of lib - er - ty,

Of thee I sing; Land where my fa - thers died, Land of the
Thy name I love; I love thy rocks and rills, Thy woods and
Sweet free-dom's song; Let mor - tal tongues a - wake, Let all that
To Thee we sing; Long may our land be bright With free-dom's

cresc.

Pil-grim's pride, From ev - 'ry moun-tain side, Let free-dom ring.
tem-pled hills, My heart with rap - ture thrills, Like that a - bove.
breathe par-take, Let rocks their si - lence break, The sound pro - long.
ho - ly light, Pro - tect us by Thy might, Great God, our King.

Maryland! My Maryland!

J.R.RANDALL

1. Thou wilt not cow - er in the dust, Ma - ry-land! my Ma - ry-land! Thy
2. Thou wilt not yield the Van-dal toll, Ma - ry-land! my Ma - ry-land! Thou
3. I see no blush up - on thy cheek, Ma - ry-land! my Ma - ry-land! Tho'
4. I hear the dis - tant thun-der hum, Ma - ry-land! my Ma - ry-land! The

gleam-ing sword shall nev - er rust, Ma - ry-land! my Ma - ry-land! Re -
wilt not crook to his con-trol, Ma - ry-land! my Ma - ry-land! Bet -
thou wast ev - er brave-ly meek, Ma - ry-land! my Ma - ry-land! For
"Old Line" bu - gle, fife, and drum, Ma - ry-land! my Ma - ry-land! Come

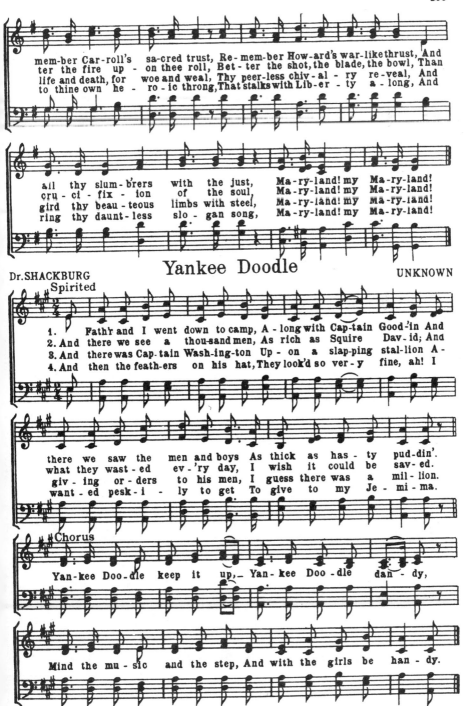

mem-ber Car-roll's sa-cred trust, Re-mem-ber How-ard's war-like thrust, And
ter the fire up - on thee roll, Bet-ter the shot, the blade, the bowl, Than
life and death, for woe and weal, Thy peer-less chiv-al - ry re-veal, And
to thine own he - ro-ic throng, That stalks with Lib-er-ty a - long, And

all thy slum-b'rers with the just, Ma-ry-land! my Ma-ry-land!
cru-ci-fix-ion of the soul, Ma-ry-land! my Ma-ry-land!
gird thy beau-teous limbs with steel, Ma-ry-land! my Ma-ry-land!
ring thy daunt-less slo-gan song, Ma-ry-land! my Ma-ry-land!

Yankee Doodle

Dr. SHACKBURG   UNKNOWN

Spirited

1. Fath'r and I went down to camp, A-long with Cap-tain Good-'in And
2. And there we see a thou-sand men, As rich as Squire Dav-id; And
3. And there was Cap-tain Wash-ing-ton Up-on a slap-ping stal-lion A-
4. And then the feath-ers on his hat, They look'd so ver-y fine, ah! I

there we saw the men and boys As thick as has-ty pud-din'.
what they wast-ed ev-'ry day, I wish it could be sav-ed.
giv-ing or-ders to his men, I guess there was a mil-lion.
want-ed pesk-i-ly to get To give to my Je-mi-ma.

Chorus

Yan-kee Doo-dle keep it up,— Yan-kee Doo-dle dan-dy,

Mind the mu-sic and the step, And with the girls be han-dy.

Battle Hymn Of The Republic

JULIA WARD HOWE

FOLK MELODY

Marcial

1. Mine eyes have seen the glo - ry of the com-ing of the Lord; He is
2. I have seen Him in the watch-fires of a hun-dred cir-cling camps; They have
3. I have read a fie-ry gos-pel, writ in bur-nish'd rows of steel; "As ye
4. He has sound-ed forth the trum-pet that shall nev-er call re-treat; He is
5. In the beau-ty of the lil - ies, Christ was born a-cross the sea, With a

tramp-ling out the vin -tage where the grapes of wrath are stored; He hath
build-ed Him an al - tar in the eve - ning dews and damps; I can
deal with my con-tem-ners, so with you my grace shall deal; Let the
sift - ing out the hearts of men be - fore his judg-ment seat; Oh, be
glo - ry in His bos - om that trans-fig-ures you and me; As He

loosed the fate - ful light-ning of His ter - ri - ble swift sword, His truth is march-ing on.
read His right-eous sen-tence by the dim and flar-ing lamps. His day is march-ing on.
He - ro, born of wo-man, crush the ser-pent with His heel, Since God is march-ing on."
swift, my soul, to an-swer Him! be ju - bi-lant my feet! Our God is march-ing on.
died to make men ho - ly, let us die to make men free, While God is march-ing on.

Chorus

Glo - ry! glo - ry! Hal - le - lu - jah! Glo-ry! glo-ry! Hal-le - lu - jah!

Glo - ry! glo-ry! Hal - le - lu - jah! His truth is march-ing on.

Columbia, The Gem Of The Ocean

THOMAS A. BECKET

Maestoso

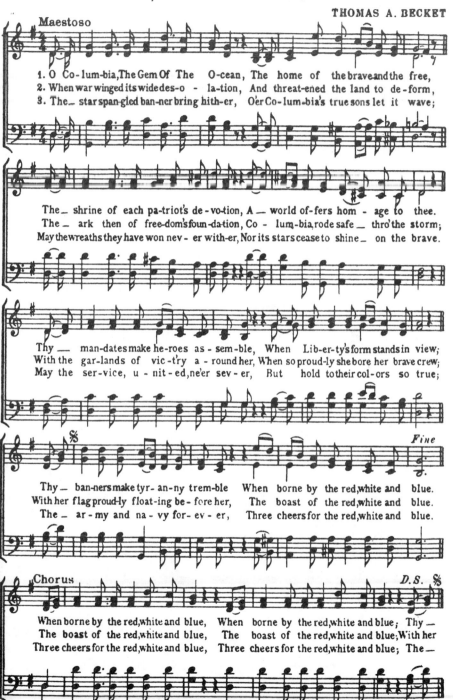

1. O Co-lum-bia, The Gem Of The O-cean, The home of the brave and the free,
2. When war winged its wide des-o - la-tion, And threat-ened the land to de-form,
3. The_ star span-gled ban-ner bring hith-er, O'er Co-lum-bia's true sons let it wave;

The_ shrine of each pa-triot's de -vo-tion, A _ world of-fers hom - age to thee.
The _ ark then of free-dom's foun-da-tion, Co - lum-bia rode safe _ thro' the storm;
May the wreaths they have won nev - er with-er, Nor its stars cease to shine_ on the brave.

Thy __ man-dates make he-roes as - sem-ble, When Lib-er-ty's form stands in view;
With the gar-lands of vic-t'ry a - round her, When so proud-ly she bore her brave crew;
May the ser-vice, u - nit-ed, ne'er sev - er, But hold to their col-ors so true;

Fine

Thy _ ban-ners make tyr- an-ny trem-ble When borne by the red, white and blue.
With her flag proud-ly float-ing be- fore her, The boast of the red, white and blue.
The _ ar - my and na - vy for- ev - er, Three cheers for the red, white and blue.

Chorus

D.S.

When borne by the red, white and blue, When borne by the red, white and blue; Thy _
The boast of the red, white and blue, The boast of the red, white and blue; With her
Three cheers for the red, white and blue, Three cheers for the red, white and blue; The_

JOSEPH HOPKINSON

Hail, Columbia!

Attributed to PHILIP PHILE

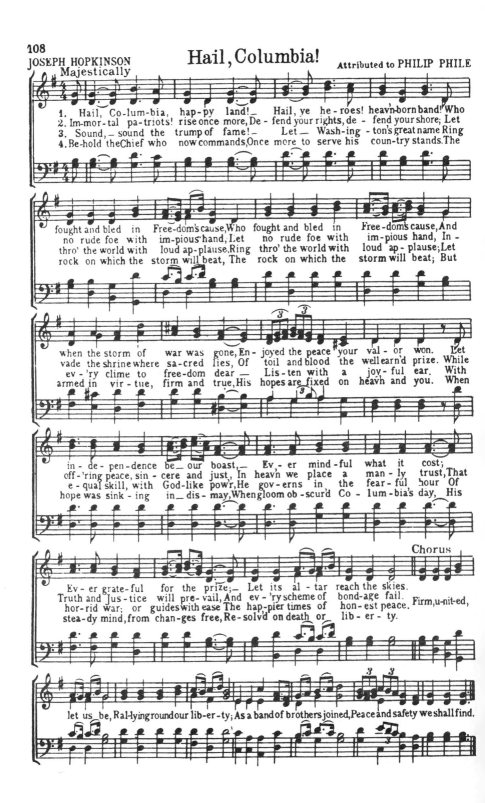

Majestically

1. Hail, Co-lum-bia, hap-py land!_ Hail, ye he-roes! heav'n-born band! Who
2. Im-mor-tal pa-triots! rise once more, De-fend your rights, de-fend your shore; Let
3. Sound,_ sound the trump of fame!_ Let_ Wash-ing-ton's great name Ring
4. Be-hold the Chief who now commands, Once more to serve his coun-try stands. The

fought and bled in Free-dom's cause, Who fought and bled in Free-dom's cause, And
no rude foe with im-pious hand, Let no rude foe with im-pious hand, In-
thro' the world with loud ap-plause, Ring thro' the world with loud ap-plause; Let
rock on which the storm will beat, The rock on which the storm will beat; But

when the storm of war was gone, En-joyed the peace your val-or won. Let
vade the shrine where sa-cred lies, Of toil and blood the well earn'd prize. While
ev-'ry clime to free-dom dear_ Lis-ten with a joy-ful ear. With
armed in vir-tue, firm and true, His hopes are fixed on heav'n and you. When

in-de-pen-dence be_ our boast,_ Ev-er mind-ful what it cost;
off-'ring peace, sin-cere and just, In heav'n we place a man-ly trust, That
e-qual skill, with God-like pow'r, He gov-erns in the fear-ful hour Of
hope was sink-ing in_ dis-may, When gloom ob-scur'd Co-lum-bia's day, His

Chorus

Ev-er grate-ful for the prize;_ Let its al-tar reach the skies.
Truth and Jus-tice will pre-vail, And ev-'ry scheme of bond-age fail. Firm, u-nit-ed,
hor-rid war; or guides with ease The hap-pier times of hon-est peace.
stea-dy mind, from chan-ges free, Re-solv'd on death or lib-er-ty.

let us be, Ral-lying round our lib-er-ty; As a band of brothers joined, Peace and safety we shall find.

Tramp! Tramp! Tramp!

GEO. F. ROOT

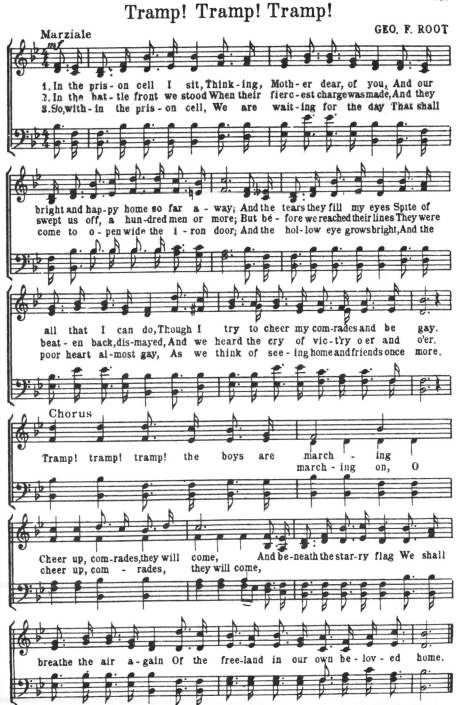

Marziale
mf

1. In the pris-on cell I sit, Think-ing, Moth-er dear, of you, And our
2. In the bat-tle front we stood When their fierc-est charge was made, And they
3. So, with-in the pris-on cell, We are wait-ing for the day That shall

bright and hap-py home so far a-way; And the tears they fill my eyes Spite of
swept us off, a hun-dred men or more; But be-fore we reached their lines They were
come to o-pen wide the i-ron door; And the hol-low eye grows bright, And the

all that I can do, Though I try to cheer my com-rades and be gay.
beat-en back, dis-mayed, And we heard the cry of vic-t'ry o er and o'er.
poor heart al-most gay, As we think of see-ing home and friends once more.

Chorus

Tramp! tramp! tramp! the boys are march - ing
march - ing on, O

Cheer up, com-rades, they will come, And be-neath the star-ry flag We shall
cheer up, com - rades, they will come,

breathe the air a-gain Of the free-land in our own be-lov-ed home.

JOHN HENRY NEWMAN

Lead, Kindly Light

JOHN B. DYKES

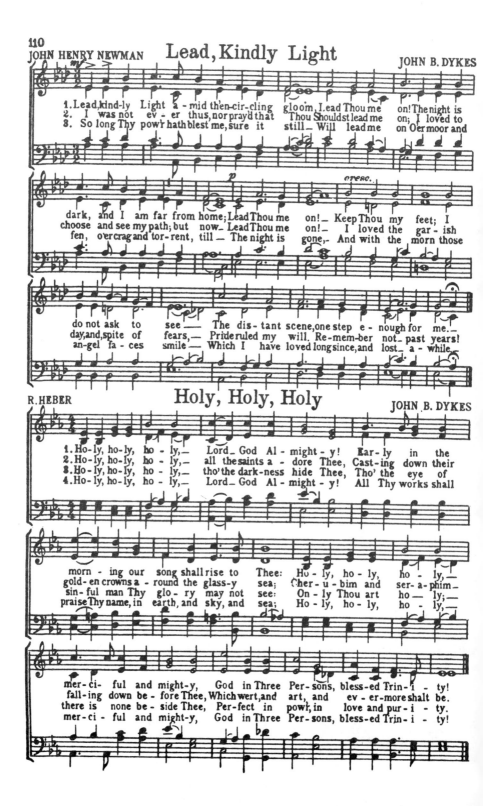

1. Lead, kind-ly Light a - mid th'en-cir-cling gloom, Lead Thou me on! The night is
2. I was not ev - er thus, nor pray'd that Thou Shouldst lead me on; I loved to
3. So long Thy pow'r hath blest me, sure it still — Will lead me on O'er moor and

dark, and I am far from home; Lead Thou me on!— Keep Thou my feet; I
choose and see my path; but now— Lead Thou me on!— I loved the gar - ish
fen, o'er crag and tor - rent, till — The night is gone,— And with the morn those

do not ask to see —— The dis - tant scene, one step e - nough for me.—
day, and, spite of fears,— Pride ruled my will. Re-mem-ber not past years!
an-gel fa - ces smile — Which I have loved long since, and lost a - while.—

R. HEBER

Holy, Holy, Holy

JOHN B. DYKES

1. Ho-ly, ho-ly, ho - ly,— Lord— God Al - might - y! Ear-ly in the
2. Ho-ly, ho-ly, ho - ly,— all the saints a - dore Thee, Cast-ing down their
3. Ho-ly, ho-ly, ho - ly,— tho' the dark-ness hide Thee, Tho' the eye of
4. Ho-ly, ho-ly, ho - ly,— Lord— God Al - might - y! All Thy works shall

morn - ing our song shall rise to Thee: Ho - ly, ho - ly, ho - ly,—
gold-en crowns a - round the glass-y sea; Cher - u - bim and ser-a-phim—
sin-ful man Thy glo - ry may not see: On - ly Thou art ho - ly;—
praise Thy name, in earth, and sky, and sea; Ho - ly, ho - ly, ho - ly,—

mer - ci - ful and might-y, God in Three Per - sons, bless-ed Trin - i - ty!
fall-ing down be - fore Thee, Which wert, and art, and ev - er-more shalt be.
there is none be - side Thee, Per-fect in pow'r, in love and pur - i - ty.
mer - ci - ful and might-y, God in Three Per - sons, bless-ed Trin - i - ty!

Onward, Christian Soldiers

SABINE BARING-GOULD

SIR ARTHUR SEYMOUR SULLIVAN

1. On-ward, Chris-tian Sol-diers! March-ing as to war, With the cross of Je-sus
2. Crowns and thrones may per - ish, King-doms rise and wane, But the Church of Je-sus
3. On-ward, then, ye peo - ple! Join our hap-py throng, Blend with ours your voic-es

Go-ing on be - fore; Christ, the roy-al Mas-ter, Leads a-gainst the foe;
Con-stant will re - main; Gates of hell can nev - er Gainst that Church pre - vail;
In the tri-umph-song; Glo - ry, laud, and hon = or Un - to Christ the King.

Chorus

For-ward in - to bat-tle, See, His ban-ners go! On-ward, Chris-tian sol - diers!
We have Christ's own pro-mise, And that can-not fail.
This thro'count-less a - ges Men and ang-els sing.

March-ing as to war, With the cross of Je-sus Go - ing on be - fore.

SARAH F. ADAMS
Nearer, My God, To Thee
LOWELL MASON

Slowly

1. Near-er, My God, To Thee, Near-er to Thee! E'en tho' it be a cross
2. Tho' like the wan-der-er, The sun gone down, Dark-ness be o - ver me,
3. There let the way ap-pear Steps un - to heav'n; All that Thou send-est me
4. Or if on joy-ful wing Cleav-ing the sky, Sun, moon, and stars for - got,

D.S. Near-er, My God, To Thee,

Fine

That rais-eth me — Still all my song shall be, Near-er, My God, To Thee,
My_ rest a stone, Yet in my dreams I'd be, Near-er, My God, To Thee,
In - mer - cy giv'n; An-gels to beck-on me, Near-er, My God, To Thee,
Up-ward I fly, – Still all my song shall be, Near-er, My God, To Thee,

D.S.

Near - er to Thee.

112

Come, Thou Almighty King

CHARLES WESLEY — FELICE GIARDINI

1. Come, Thou al - might - y King, Help us Thy name to sing, Help us to praise! Fa - ther all - glo - ri - ous, O'er all vic - to - ri - ous, Come and reign o - ver us, An-cient of days!
2. Come, Thou in - car - nate Word, Gird on Thy might - y sword, Our prayer at - tend! Come, and Thy peo - ple bless, And give Thy word suc-cess· Spir - it of ho - li - ness, On us de - scend!
3. Come, Ho - ly Com - fort - er, Thy sa - cred wit - ness bear, In this glad hour! Thou, who al - might - y art, Now rule in ev-'ry heart, And ne'er from us de-part,Spir-it of pow'r!

Abide With Me

HENRY F. LYTE — WILLIAM H. MONK

1. A-bide With Me! Fast falls the e - ven - tide, The dark - ness deep - ens Lord, with me a - bide! When oth - er help - ers fail, and com-forts flee, Help of the help-less, oh, A-bide With Me!
2. Swift to its close ebbs out life's lit - tle day; Earth's joys grow dim, its glo - ries pass a - way; Change and de - cay in all a - round I see; O Thou, who chang-est not, A-bide With Me!
3. I need Thy pres-ence ev - 'ry pass-ing hour; What but Thy grace can foil the temp-ter's pow'r? Who, like Thy - self, my guide and stay can be? Through cloud and sun-shine,Lord, A-bide With Me!

Praise God From Whom All Blessings Flow
(Old Hundreth - The Doxology)
LOUIS BOURGEOIS

Praise God, From Whom All Bless-ings Flow; Praise Him, all creat-ures here be-low;

Praise Him a-bove, ye heavn-ly host; Praise Fa-ther, Son and Ho-ly Ghost.

JOHN FAWCETT
Blest Be The Tie That Binds
HANS G. NAGELI

1. Blest Be The Tie That Binds Our hearts in Christ-ian love;
2. Be - fore our Fa - ther's throne. We pour our ar - dent pray'rs;
3. We share our mu - tual woes, Our mu - tual bur - dens bear;
4. When we a - sun - der part, It gives us in - ward pain;

The fel - low - ship of kin - dred minds Is like to that a - bove.
Our fears, our hopes, our aims are one, Our com-forts and our cares.
And oft - en for each oth - er flows The sym - pa - thiz - ing tear.
But we shall still be joined in heart, And hope to meet a - gain.

The Lord's Prayer
Recitativo
SACRED CHANT

Our Father who art in Heav'n Hallowed be Thy name.
Give us this day our dai - ly bread.
And lead us not into temptation; But deliver us from evil,

Thy kingdom come, Thy will be done on earth as it is in Heaven.
And forgive us our tresspasses, As we forgive those who tresspass a-gainst us.
For Thine is the kingdom, And the power, and the glory for ever and ever A - men.

Rock Of Ages

AUGUSTUS M. TOPLADY

THOMAS HASTINGS

1. Rock Of A - ges, cleft for me, Let me hide my - self in Thee;
2. Could my tears for - ev - er flow, Could my zeal no lan - guor know,
3. While I draw this fleet-ing breath, When my eyes shall close in death,

Let the wa - ter and the blood, From Thy wound - ed side which flowed,
These for sin could not a - tone; Thou must save, and Thou a - lone;
When I rise to worlds un - known, And be - hold Thee on Thy throne,

Be of sin the dou - ble cure, Save from wrath and make me pure.
In my hand no price I bring; Sim - ply to Thy cross I cling.
Rock Of A - ges, cleft for me, Let me hide my-self in Thee.

How Can I Leave Thee

Moderately

THURINGIAN FOLKSONG

1. How Can I Leave Thee! How can I from thee part! Thou, on - ly,
2. Blue is a flow-'ret Called the "For - get - me - not," Wear it up -
3. Would I a bird were, Soon at thy side to be! Fal - con nor

hath my heart, Dear one be-lieve. Thou hath this soul of mine, So close-ly
on thy heart, And think of me! Flow-'ret and hope may die, Yet love with
hawk would fear, Speed-ing to thee. When by the fow-ler slain, I at thy

bound to thine, No oth - er can I love, Save thee a - lone!
us shall stay, That can - not pass a - way, Dear one be - lieve.
feet should lie, Thou sad - ly shouldst com-plain, Joy- ful I'd die!

116

Adeste Fideles
(O Come, All Ye Faithful)

Brightly

JOHN READING

1. O Come, All Ye Faith-ful Joy-ful and tri-um-phant, O come ye, O come ye to
2. Sing choirs of An-gels, Sing in ex-ul-ta-tion, Sing all ye ci-tiz-ens of

A-des-te, Fi-de-les, Lae-ti tri-um-phan-tes, Ve-ni-te, ve-ni-te, in

Beth'-le-hem. Come and be-hold Him, Born the King of An-gels: O come, let us a-
heav'n a-bove: Glo-ry to God,__ In the High-est, glo-ry! O come, let us a-

Beth-le-hem. Na-tum vi-de-te, Re-gem an-ge-lo-rum. Ve-ni-te, a-do-

dore Him, O come, let us a-dore Him, O come, let us a-dore Him, Christ the Lord.

re-mus, Ve-ni-te, a-do-re-mus. Ve-ni-te a-do-re-mus Do-mi-num.

ISAAC WATTS

Joy To The World

GEORGE F. HANDEL

Broad

1. Joy To The World! the Lord is come; Let earth re-ceive her King;__ Let
2. Joy To The World! the Sav-ior reigns; Let men their songs em-ploy;__ While
3. No more let sin and sor-row grow, Nor thorns in-fest the ground; He
4. He rules the world with truth and grace, And makes the na-tions prove__ The

ev-'ry heart pre-pare Him room, And heav'n and na-ture sing, And
fields and floods, rocks, hills and plains, Re-peat the sound-ing joy, Re-
comes to make__ His bless-ings flow Far as the curse is found, Far
glo-ries of__ His right-eous-ness, And won-ders of his love, And

And heav'n, and heav'n and na-ture

heav'n and na-ture sing, And heav'n, and heav'n and na-ture sing.
peat the sound-ing joy, Re-peat,__ re-peat__ the sound-ing joy.
as the curse is found, Far as,__ far as__ the curse is found.
won-ders of His love, And wonders, and won-ders of His love.

sing, And heav'n and na-ture sing,

Nobody Knows The Trouble I've Had

Slowly

AMERICAN NEGRO SPIRITUAL

No-bod-y Knows The Trou-ble I've Had, No-bod-y knows but Je-sus.

No-bod-y Knows The Trou-ble I've Had Glo-ry Hal-le-lu-jah!

Some-times I'm up, some-times I'm down, Oh, yes, Lord.— Some-
I nev-er shall for-get that day, Oh, yes, Lord.— When

times I'm al-most to the ground Oh, yes, Lord.—
Je-sus washed my sins a-way Oh, yes, Lord.—

Brothers

As a band of Broth-ers joined, One in heart and one in mind, Peace and safe-ty we shall find.

Deep River

AMERICAN NEGRO SPIRITUAL

Deep River my home is o-ver Jor-dan, Deep River, Lord, I want to cross o-ver in-to camp-ground. Deep, deep River my home is o-ver Jor-dan Deep, deep River, Lord, I want to cross o-ver in-to camp-ground.

Heav'n, Heav'n
(All God's Children)

AMERICAN NEGRO SPIRITUAL

1. I've got a robe, You've got a robe, All God's chil-dren got a robe;
2. I've got a crown, You've got a crown, All God's chil-dren got a crown;
3. I've got a song, You've got a song, All God's chil-dren got a song,

When I get to Heaven goin' to put on my robe, Goin' to shout all o-ver God's Heav'n-
When I get to Heaven goin' to put on my crown, Goin' to shout all o-ver God's Heav'n-
When I get to Heaven goin' to sing a new song, Goin' to sing all o-ver God's Heav'n-

Swing Low, Sweet Chariot

NEGRO SPIRITUAL

Heav'n — Heav'n — Ev'-ry-bod-y talk-in''bout Heav'n ain't go-in' there

Heav'n — Heav'n — Goin' to shout all o-ver God's Heav'n.

Swing Low, Sweet Char-i-ot,— Com-in' for to car-ry me home! Swing Low, Sweet

Char-i-ot, Com-in' for to car-ry me home!

1. I looked o-ver Jor-dan and
2. If you get—there be-
3. I'm some-times— up and—

what did I see,— Com-in' for to car-ry me home! A
fore— I do,— Com-in' for to car-ry me home! Tell
some-times down, Com-in' for to car-ry me home! But

band of an-gels com-in' af-ter me, Com-in' for to car-ry me home!
all my friends that I'm— com-in' too, Com-in' for to car-ry me home!
still my soul feels heav-en-ly bound, Com-in' for to car-ry me home!

120

The Old Gray Mare

Oh, The Old Gray Mare, She ain't what she used to be, Ain't what she used to be, Ain't what she used to be. The Old Gray Mare, She ain't what she used to be, Man-y long years a - go.

Man-y long years a - go Man-y long years a - go. Oh, The

Hand Me Down My Walkin' Cane

Moderately fast   Male Voices

1. Hand Me Down ____ My Walk - in' Cane, ____ Hand Me
2. Hand me down ____ my bot-tle o' corn, ____ Hand me

Down ____ My Walk - in' Cane. ____ Oh!
down ____ my bot - tle o' corn. ____ Oh!

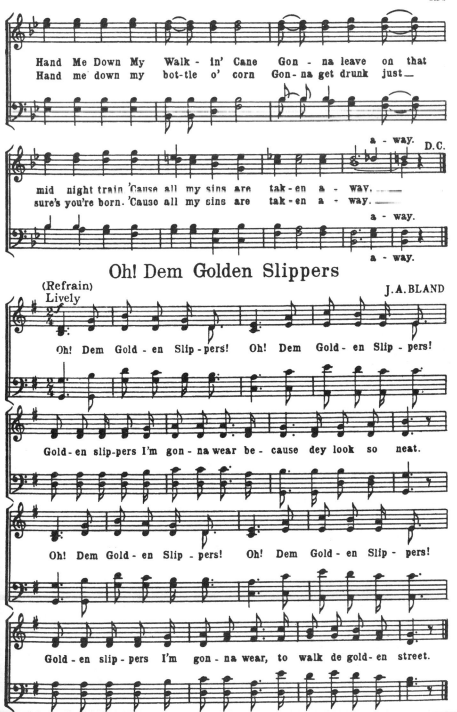

Hand Me Down My Walk - in' Cane Gon - na leave on that
Hand me down my bot-tle o' corn Gon-na get drunk just—

mid night train 'Cause all my sins are tak-en a - way.
sure's you're born. 'Cause all my sins are tak-en a - way.
a - way.
a - way.
a - way.
D.C.

Oh! Dem Golden Slippers

J.A.BLAND

(Refrain)
Lively

Oh! Dem Gold - en Slip-pers! Oh! Dem Gold- en Slip - pers!

Gold-en slip-pers I'm gon - na wear be - cause dey look so neat.

Oh! Dem Gold - en Slip - pers! Oh! Dem Gold - en Slip - pers!

Gold - en slip - pers I'm gon - na wear, to walk de gold- en street.

Jingle Bells

J. PIERPONT

Brightly

1. Dash - ing thro' the snow In a one - horse o - pen sleigh, And
2. Day or two a - go I __ thought I'd take a ride, And
3. Now the ground is white, Go it while you're young;

O'er the fields we go, Laugh - ing all the way; The
soon Miss Fan - nie Bright Was seat - ed by my side; Just
Take the girls to - night, And sing this sleigh - ing song;

Bells on bob - tail ring, Mak - ing spir - its bright; What
horse was lean and lank, Mis - for - tune seem'd his lot, He
get a bob-tailed nag, Two - for - ty for his speed, Then

fun it is to ride and sing A sleigh - ing song to - night!
got in - to a drift - ed bank, And we, we got up - sot.
hitch him to an o - pen sleigh, And crack! you'll take the lead.

Refrain *(Accompanied by jingling glasses)*

Jin-gle Bells! Jin-gle Bells! Jin-gle all the way! Oh, what fun it is to ride

1.
In a one-horse o - pen sleigh!

2.
In a one-horse o - pen sleigh!

She'll Be Comin' 'Round The Mountain
(When She Comes)

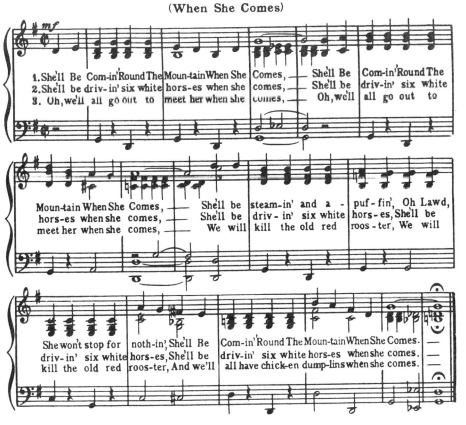

1. She'll Be Com-in' Round The Moun-tain When She Comes, — She'll Be Com-in' Round The Moun-tain When She Comes, — She'll be steam-in' and a - puf-fin', Oh Lawd, She won't stop for noth-in', She'll Be Com-in' Round The Moun-tain When She Comes. —

2. She'll be driv-in' six white hors-es when she comes, — She'll be driv-in' six white hors-es when she comes, — She'll be driv-in' six white hors-es, She'll be driv-in' six white hors-es, She'll be driv-in' six white hors-es when she comes. —

3. Oh, we'll all go out to meet her when she comes, — Oh, we'll all go out to meet her when she comes, — We will kill the old red roos-ter, We will kill the old red roos-ter, And we'll all have chick-en dump-lins when she comes. —

Where Is My Little Dog Gone?

Allegro

Oh where, Oh Where Is My Lit-tle Dog Gone, Oh where, oh where can he be? With his ears cut short and his tail cut long, Oh where, oh where is he.

Landlord, Fill The Flowing Bowl

1. Come, Land-lord, Fill The Flow-ing Bowl, Un - til it doth run o - ver, Come,
2. The man that drinks good whis - ky punch, And goes to bed right mel - low, The
3. The man who drinks cold wa - ter pure, And goes to bed quite so - ber, The
4. But he who drinks just what he likes, And get-teth "half seas o - ver," But
5. The pret-ty girl that gets a kiss, And goes and tells her moth-er, The

Land-lord, Fill The Flow-ing Bowl, Un - til it doth run o - ver,
man that drinks good whis - ky punch, And goes to bed right mel - low,
man who drinks cold wa - ter pure, And goes to bed quite so - ber,
he who drinks just what he likes, And get - teth "half seas o - ver,"
pret - ty girl that gets a kiss, And goes and tells her moth - er,

Chorus

For to-night we'll mer-ry, mer-ry be, For to-night we'll mer-ry, mer-ry be,
Lives as he ought to live, Lives as he ought to live,
Falls as the leaves do fall, Falls as the leaves do fall,
Will live un - til he dies, Will live un - til he dies,
Does a ver - y fool - ish thing, Does a ver - y fool - ish thing,

For to-night we'll mer-ry, mer-ry be, To - mor-row we'll be so - ber.
Lives as he ought to live, And dies a jol - ly fel - low.
Falls as the leaves do fall, So rare - ly in Oc - to - ber.
Will live un - til he dies, per-haps, And then lie down in clo - ver.
Does a ver - y fool - ish thing, And don't de - serve an - oth - er.

Whoa, Emma!

JOHN READ

Moderately

1. I don't mind tell-ing you, I took my girl to Kew, And Em-ma was the
2. I asked them what they meant? When some-one at me sent, An egg which near-ly
3. An old man said to me, "Why, young man can't you see the joke, and I looked

dar-ling crea-ture's name; — While stand-ing on the pier, Some
struck me in the eye. — The girl be-gan to scream, Say-ing
at him with sur - prise, — He said "Don't be put out, It's a

her name.
the eye.
sur - prise.

chaps at her did leer, And one and all a -round her did ex - claim: —
"Fred what does this mean?" I asked a-gain and this was their re - ply: —
say - ing got a - bout "And then their voic-es seemed to rend the skies. —

Refrain -Waltz-time

Whoa, Em-ma! Whoa, Em-ma! Em-ma you put me in quite a di - lem-ma!

Oh, Em-ma! Whoa, Em-ma! That's what I heard from Put-ney to Kew.

The Spanish Cavalier

W.D.H.

W. D. HENDRICKSON

Moderato

1. A Span-ish Cav-a-lier stood in his re-treat, And on his gui-tar played a tune, dear; The mu-sic so sweet, Would oft-times re-peat The bless-ing of my coun-try and you, dear.

2. I'm off to the war, to the war I must go, To fight for my coun-try and you, dear; But if I should fall, In vain I would call, The bless-ing of my coun-try and you, dear.

3. And when the war is o'er, to you I'll re-turn, A gain to my coun-try and you, dear; But if I be slain, You may seek me in vain, Up-on the bat-tle-field you will find me.

Chorus

Oh, say, dar-ling, say, when I'm far a-way, Some-times you may think of me dear; Bright sun-ny days will soon fade a-way, Re-mem-ber what I say, and be true, dear.

Come, Let's Sing A Merry Round

Come, Let's Sing A Mer-ry Round, Wake the cheer-ful, cheer-ful glee;

Glad-ly let our voic-es sound: Oh hap-py, hap-py we, hap-py we.

Where Did You Get That Hat

JOS. J. SULLIVAN

Where Did You Get That Hat? Where did you get that tile?

Is - n't it a nob - by one, and just the prop - er style?

I should like to have one just the same as that! Wher -

e're I go they shout "Hel - lo! Where Did You Get That Hat?"

The Bowery

PERCY GAUNT

CHARLES A. HOYT

Waltz tempo (*very marked*)

The Bow - 'ry, The Bow - 'ry; They say such things and they do strange

things on The Bow - 'ry, The Bow - 'ry, I'll nev-er go there an-y more.

Sweet Marie

C. WARMAN

RAYMOND MOORE

Moderato

Come to me, Sweet Ma - rie, Sweet Ma - rie, come to me, Not be-cause your face is fair, love, to see. ___ But your soul so pure and sweet Makes my hap - pi - ness com-plete, Makes me fal - ter at your feet, Sweet Ma - rie. ___

to — see.

rall.

Sing Again That Sweet Refrain

Waltz time *(Slowly)*

GUSSIE L. DAVIS

Sing A - gain That Sweet Re - frain; "Dars where the old folks stay;" It takes me back to slav-'ry days, Be - fore I was sold a-way, ___ A - long de Swan-nee Riv - er banks, Dars where I

It takes me back, back to

sold a - way — A - long

Oh,

She Was Happy 'Till She Met You

CHARLES GRAHAM   MONROE ROSENFELD

Little Annie Rooney

Refrain - Waltz time

MICHAEL NOLAN

She's my sweet-heart, I'm her beau; — She's my An-nie, — I'm her Joe, — Soon we'll mar-ry, — Nev-er — to part, — Lit-tle An-nie Roon-ey — is my sweet-heart! —

Nev - er

She May Have Seen Better Days

Slowly

JAMES THORNTON

She May Have Seen Bet-ter Days, — When she was in her

Bet - ter Days

prime; — She May Have Seen Bet-ter Days —

(in her prime)

Once up -

Once up - on a time _____ Tho' by the way-side she
(once up - on a time)

on a

fell, ___ She may yet mend her ways,(mend her ways. _)

Some poor old moth-er is wait-ing for her,Who has seen bet-ter days. _

Daisy Bell
(Bicycle Built For Two)

HARRY DACRE

Waltz tempo

Dai - sy, Dai - sy, Give me your an-swer, do ___ I'm half

cra - zy All for the love of you. __ It won't be a styl - ish mar-riage;_ I can't af-

ford a car-riage,_ But you'll look sweet on a seat of a bi-cy-cle built for two.

I Don't Want To Play In Your Yard

PHILIP WINGATE

H.W. PETRIE

Slow waltz tempo

I Don't Want To Play In Your Yard, I don't like you an-y more

You'll be sor-ry when you see me Slid-ing down our cel-lar door.

You can't hol-ler down our rain-barrel, You can't climb our ap-ple tree.

I Don't Want To Play In Your Yard, If you won't be good to me.

Just Tell Them That You Saw Me

PAUL DRESSER

Slowly

Male Voices

"Just Tell Them That You Saw Me" She said,"They'll know the rest; Just

tell them I was look-ing well, you know; — Just

whisp- er, if you get a chance, to moth-er dear and say ____ "I

and say

love her as I did long, long a - go. Long, long a - go.

Comrades

FELIX McGLENNON

Waltz time

Com - rades, Com - rades, ev-er since we were boys. ____

Shar-ing each oth-er's sor - rows, Shar-ing each oth-er's joys; ____

Com-rades when man-hood was dawn - ing, Faith-ful what e'er may be-tide; ____

When dan-ger threat-ened my jol-ly old Com-rade was there by my side. ____

When The Robins Nest Again

FRANK HOWARD

When The Rob-ins Nest A - gain, ___ And the flow-ers are in bloom. ___ (are in bloom.) When the spring-time's sun-ny smile ___ Seems to ban-ish all sor-row and gloom (and gloom) Then my bon-nie blue-eyed lad _____ If my heart is true 'till then. ___ (un-til then) Has prom-ised he'll re-turn to me, When The Rob-ins Nest A - gain.

Wait Till The Clouds Roll By

Refrain

H. T. FULMER

Moderately slow

Wait Till The Clouds Roll By, Jen-ny, Wait Till The Clouds Roll By, Jen-ny, my own true loved one, Wait Till The Clouds Roll By.

rall.

My Sweetheart's The Man In The Moon

JAMES THORNTON

Waltz tempo (marcato)

My Sweet-heart's The Man In The Moon ____ I'm go-ing to mar-ry him soon, ____ 'Twould fill me with bliss just to give him one kiss, But I know that a doz-en I nev-er would miss, I'll go up in a great big bal - loon ____ And see my sweet-heart in the moon, ____ Then be-hind a dark cloud where no one is al - low'd, I'll make love to the Man In The Moon.

The Band Played On

CHARLES WARD

Waltz time (*with a swing*)

Ca-sey would waltz with a straw-ber-ry blonde, And The Band Played On ———— He'd glide 'cross the floor with the girl he a-dored, And The Band Played On ———— But his brain was so load-ed it near-ly ex-plod-ed, The poor girl would shake with a-larm. ———— He'd ne'er leave the girl with the straw-ber-ry curls And The Band Played On. ————

with a - larm.

The More We Get Together

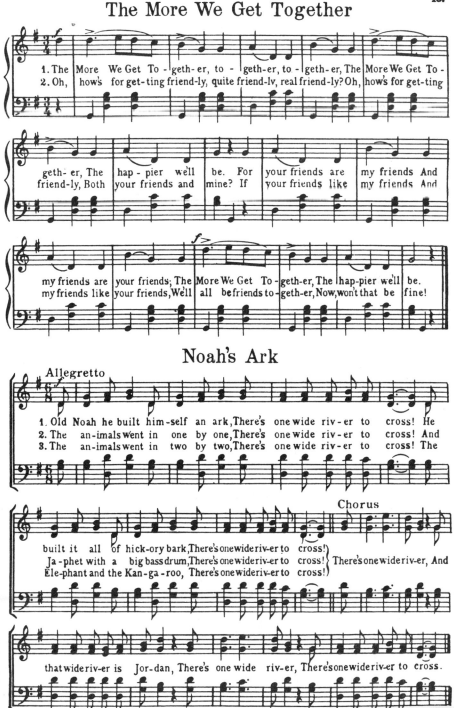

1. The More We Get To - geth- er, to - geth- er, to - geth- er, The More We Get To - geth- er, The hap - pier we'll be. For your friends are my friends And my friends are your friends; The More We Get To - geth- er, The hap-pier we'll be.

2. Oh, how's for get-ting friend-ly, quite friend-ly, real friend-ly? Oh, how's for get-ting friend-ly, Both your friends and mine? If your friends like my friends And my friends like your friends, We'll all be friends to-geth-er, Now, won't that be fine!

Noah's Ark

Allegretto

1. Old Noah he built him-self an ark, There's one wide riv-er to cross! He built it all of hick-ory bark, There's one wide riv-er to cross!

2. The an-imals went in one by one, There's one wide riv-er to cross! And Ja-phet with a big bass drum, There's one wide riv-er to cross!

3. The an-imals went in two by two, There's one wide riv-er to cross! The Ele-phant and the Kan-ga-roo, There's one wide riv-er to cross!

Chorus

There's one wide riv-er, And that wide riv-er is Jor-dan, There's one wide riv-er, There's one wide riv-er to cross.

How D'ye Do?

In Style All The While

* Use name as occasion demands.

Happy Are We Tonight

M. S. PIKE

Lively

1. Hap-py Are We To - night, boys Hap-py, hap-py are we; The hearts that we de-
2. Man-y will be the mile, boys Man-y, man-y the mile, That we shall rove and

light boys, With us may hap-py be. _ Friends may laugh with those who laugh, And
smile boys, With those we ne'er be - guile. The voic - es we have of - ten heard, And

sigh for those in pain; The most of us have met be-fore and now we meet a - gain.
fa - ces we have met, Like tones of sweet-est mel - o - dy We nev-er can for - get.

For He's A Jolly Good Fellow

Lively

1. {For He's A Jol - ly Good Fel - low, For He's A Jol - ly Good
   {We won't go home un - til morn - ing, We won't go home un - til
2. {The bear went o - ver the moun - tain, The bear went o - ver the
   {Was the oth - er side of the moun - tain, The oth - er side of the

{Fel - low, For He's A Jol - ly Good Fel - low, Which
{morn - ing, We won't go home un - til morn - ing, Till
{moun-tain, The bear went o - ver the moun - tain, To
{moun-tain, The oth - er side of the moun - tain, Was

Fine   D.C.

{no-bod-y can de - ny, _ Which no-bod-y can de - ny.
{day_ light doth ap - pear! 'Till day_ light doth ap - pear.
{see_ what he could see! _ And all _ that he could see.
{all _ that he could see. _

Reuben And Rachel

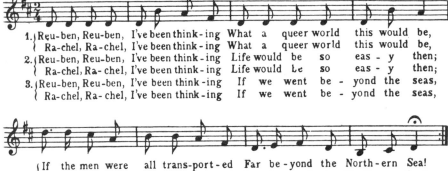

1. {Reu-ben, Reu-ben, I've been think-ing What a queer world this would be,
   { Ra-chel, Ra-chel, I've been think-ing What a queer world this would be,
2. {Reu-ben, Reu-ben, I've been think-ing Life would be so eas - y then;
   { Ra-chel, Ra-chel, I've been think-ing Life would be so eas - y then;
3. {Reu-ben, Reu-ben, I've been think-ing If we went be - yond the seas,
   { Ra-chel, Ra-chel, I've been think-ing If we went be - yond the seas,

{If the men were all trans-port-ed Far be-yond the North-ern Sea!
{If the girls were all trans-port-ed Far be-yond the North-ern Sea!
{What a love-ly world this would be If there were no tire-some men!
{What a love-ly world this would be If you'd leave it to the men!
{All the men would fol-low aft-er Like a swarm of hum-ble-bees!
{All the girls would fol-low aft-er Like a swarm of hon-ey-bees!

This may be sung as a canon by dividing the chorus into two sections. The first section, (women's voices) begins; when they have sung the first measure, the second section, (men's voices) begins and continues one measure behind the others, using the second line of each verse. It can also be used as a group duet by having the women sing the first line of each verse followed by the men with the second line.

Old MacDonald Had A Farm

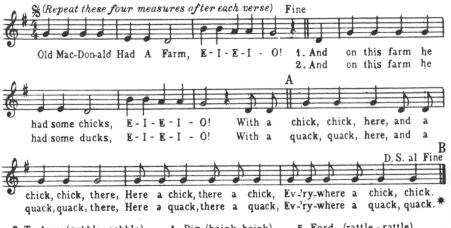

Old Mac-Don-ald Had A Farm, E - I - E - I - O! 1. And on this farm he
2. And on this farm he

had some chicks, E - I - E - I - O! With a chick, chick, here, and a
had some ducks, E - I - E - I - O! With a quack, quack, here, and a

chick, chick, there, Here a chick, there a chick, Ev-'ry-where a chick, chick.
quack, quack, there, Here a quack, there a quack, Ev-'ry-where a quack, quack.*

3. Turkey (gobble-gobble). 4. Pig (hoink-hoink). 5. Ford (rattle-rattle).

*Each stanza repeats after it has reached this point, all the material of the preceding stanzas between the letters A and B. The fifth stanza in full would be thus:

With a rattle-rattle here, etc. Hoink-hoink here, etc. Gobble-gobble here, etc. Quack-quack here, etc. Chick-chick here, etc. Old MacDonald Had A Farm, E-I-E-I-O!

142

Our Boys Will Shine Tonight
Mixed Voices

Our Boys Will Shine To-Night, Our boys will shine. Our Boys Will

Shine To-night, All down the line. They've washed their fac-es too. Out for a

time When the sun goes down And the moon comes up, Our boys will shine.

The Three Little Pigs

A. S. GATTY

1. A —— jol-ly old sow —— once lived in a sty, And
2. "My —— dear lit-tle broth-ers" said one of the brats, "My
3. Then these three lit-tle pig-gies grew skin-ny and lean, And

Three lit-tle pig-gies had she, —— And she wad-dled a-bout, say-ing
dear lit-tle pig-gies"said he, —— "Let us all for the fu-ture say
lean they might ver-y well be, —— For some-how they could-n't say

"Umph, Umph, Umph," While the lit-tle ones said "Wee, Wee."—
"Umph, Umph, Umph," 'Tis so child-ish to say Wee, Wee."—
"Umph, Umph, Umph," And they would-n't say "Wee, Wee, Wee."—

Sucking Cider Thru A Straw

1. The nic-est girl ___ I ev-er saw ___ Was Suck-ing Ci - der Thru A Straw. ___
2. And now I've got ___ a ma-in-law ___ From Suck-ing Ci - der Thru A Straw. ___

Hail! Hail! The Gang's All Here

March tempo

Hail! Hail! ___ The Gang's All Here, What the heck do we care

What the heck do we care What the heck do we care now.

Good-Night, Ladies

Male Quartette

COLLEGE SONG

1. Good-Night, La-dies! ___ Good-Night, Lá-dies! ___ Good-Night,
2. Fare-well, la-dies! ___ Fare-well, la-dies! ___ Fare-well,

La-dies! ___ We're goin' to leave you now. Mer-ri-ly we roll a-long,
la-dies! ___ We're goin' to leave you now.

Roll a-long, roll a-long, Mer-ri-ly we roll a-long, O-ver the dark blue sea.

CONTENTS